LIVING THE DREAM

*For those who have ever fallen in love with an ocean
or a sea, may the breath of salty air on your face
remain a reminder of where you want to be.*

LIVING THE DREAM

Life by the water in New Zealand

RANDOM HOUSE
NEW ZEALAND

DEREK MORRISON

CONTENTS

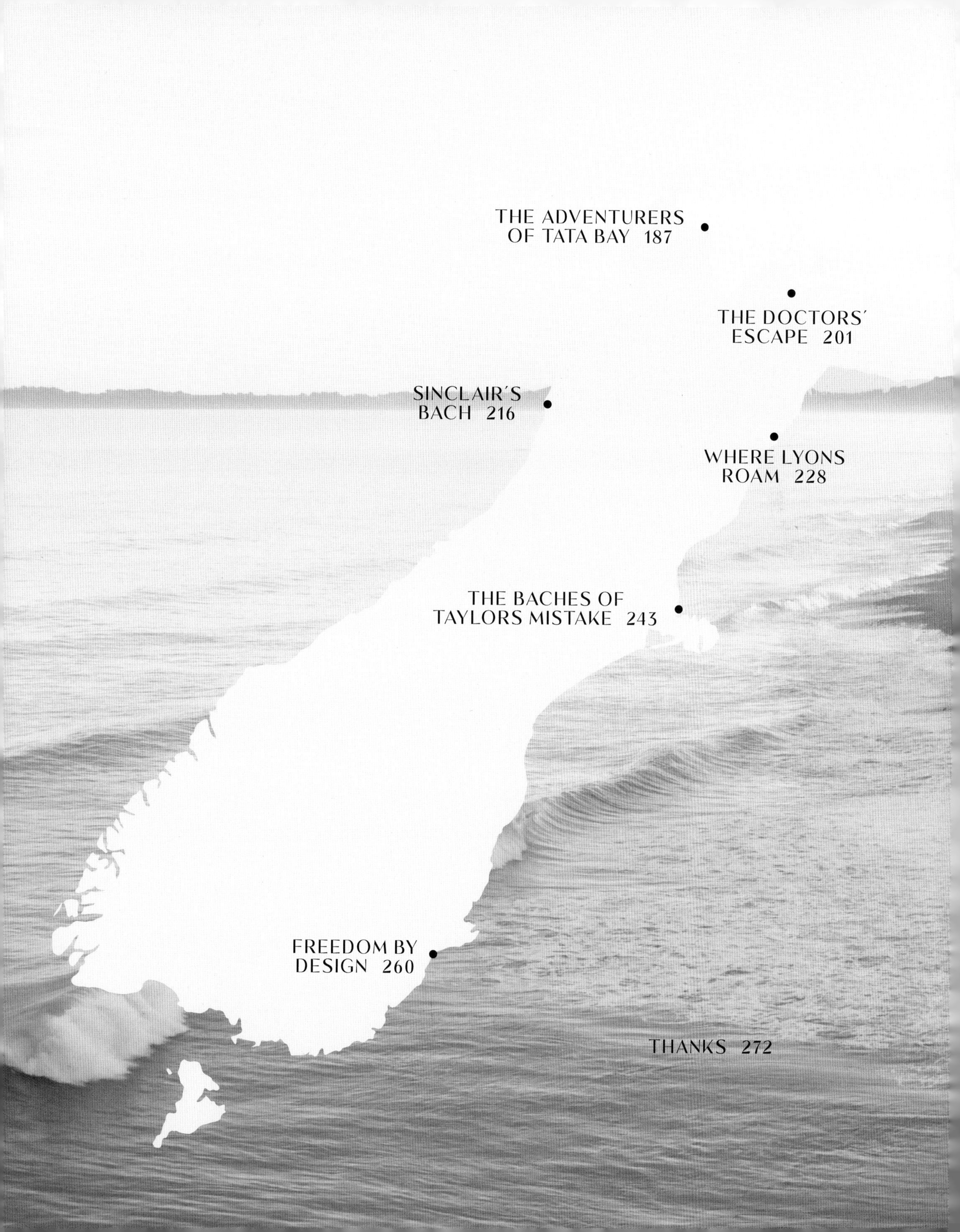

INTRODUCTION

There's a craving for escape within all New Zealanders. It thrives in that gap between our work lives and where we indulge our passions, relax and play. It's woven into our lifestyle, and the value we place on it trumps nearly everything else in our lives. For those people whose lives are connected to the coast, our rivers or our lakes, then finding a place to anchor that passion is the ultimate.

Baches — or cribs, as they are called in the south — have always been a part of the New Zealand way of life, a static embodiment of the Kiwi way. Often, they've passed through generations remarkably unchanged. Or the dwelling reaches a point of such disrepair that one generation bites the bullet and renovates from the ground up to renew the cycle. Others move in permanently to immerse themselves fully in their lifestyle. Mostly, the buildings are functional and homely, but almost never

viewed from the perspective of an investment.

They're often gathering places for extended families — places where whānau come together and share experiences, relax, and regale each other with old stories. Places that fill with laughter and create moments and traditions that endure well beyond the time spent within them.

The walls reference the history, past journeys and the lives of those who have called these places home. Each has a story that links it to its location, the environment and its people. And whether the bach is opulent, rustic or barely standing, the result does not change — money has little value when you're sharing experiences with loved ones in a part of the world that has won your heart.

Physically, the dwellings in this book vary vastly in scale and quality, but the essence of them is consistent. They capture the passion of their occupants and afford them direct access to their adventures.

While putting together the Millars of Monkey Rock chapter for this book, I met Carolyn Gundy, a celebrated architect living in a beautifully styled, near-original bach on the beachfront at North Piha. She shares it with her husband Stu and two girls, Leia and Portia. When I visited them, we met around a table that disguised a stairwell. It lay between the kitchen and the living room. It's not a huge space, but Caro's worked her magic on it. She shared something with me that resonates with each of the dwellings in this book.

PREVIOUS SPREAD
Tata Bay, Abel Tasman National Park.

ABOVE
Fiordland's west coast, near Big Bay.

OPPOSITE
Rustic, makeshift and ultimately illegal. Jason Searle's hut was dismantled and shipped out in containers in 2012.

Jason's hut had a view to one of the best surf reefs in Big Bay.

Jason's Big Bay hut, complete with wash basin and hammock bed.

'The heart of the home is that space where everybody comes together. The sun shines in and you've got those moments where people are enjoying themselves and connected to the environment. That's my biggest thing in architecture — capturing that appreciation and awareness of where you are and your sense of place. If I can achieve that, then for me that's success.'

In the context of the homes and baches throughout this book, her words echo off every page. These are places where families build traditions, memories and togetherness — often on a regular basis. They span many generations and shelter multiple generations within the same timeframe.

They're designed to expand and contract to absorb family members and friends as needed. They feature bunkrooms and sleep-outs or camping areas to accommodate the growing tribes. They're about inclusiveness and come with very few rules, but a lot of games, books and moments.

To put Caro's insightful lens on it, if the heart of a home is the space where everybody comes together, then the humble New Zealand bach is the heart of a family. It's a focal point for friends and family to meet — a base camp for adding another chapter to their shared experiences.

In many of these chapters, a Robinson Crusoe-esque theme emerges. It has filaments through all the stories — places so remote and isolated that they seem to be the stuff of childhoood dreams. They're exciting and frightening at the same time, but ultimately hitch themselves to your imaginaton.

One example, at the extreme end of the spectrum, existed for a short time near Big Bay in Fiordland. A friend of mine, Jason Searle, had found himself trapping possums in the remote bushland of the area around 2010. Searley had a permit from the Department of Conservation and he trapped

possums on a semi-regular basis — going in for anywhere from five days to two weeks — depending on the weather.

His campsite grew as he recovered resources from the rocks or ferried the odd component in, until he had something that resembled a very basic hut. Each addition made his space more comfortable, and he survived on crayfish, possums, venison and whatever he could bring in. With each trip, he became sharper at the game, until he was harvesting 10 kilos of fur in a good week, for a market that was paying $140/kilo. He reinvested the income in traps and honed his survival skills . . . and surfed the local breaks when time and conditions allowed.

From the outside, it was idyllic, the ultimate for any surfer with a dream of escape. But in reality, it was harsh: sandflies in thick clouds and weather that often swiped at his hut's very foundations. He's told me of near-misses for himself and colleagues at almost every turn and the good dose of luck that followed him.

Searley got to a point where he had wrestled with all that was thrown at him and found a wild existence, disconnected from society, but drawing from it all the same.

With time authorities deemed his hut to be more permanent than a campsite and ordered it to be removed. He broke the hut into pieces and shipped it out of Big Bay in 2012. Nothing was left behind except, for Searley at least, the knowledge not just that he could live in

Jason catches some dinner to go with a freshly killed deer he shot a day earlier.

Baylin Klein Ovink paddles towards the rising sun for a surf at Papamoa with her family.

the wild, but that he could thrive in it. Kernels of Searley's dream and ambition exist within each of the people featured within this book.

The place where we unwind and interact with nature always begins with the location. From fishing to surfing, diving to waka ama to simply exploring the coastline, it is our love for these coastal, river and lake environments that enriches our lives. They are what first attract us to a landscape and sustain that relationship throughout the years. We thrive in being immersed in these places and connecting with them.

Our memories are hinged to weather events, outstanding swells, enduring sunshine and plentiful time in the water. The promise of adventure occupies our minds, like a

familiar friend guiding you to a place of happiness. Sharing that with your loved ones only serves to intensify the excitement and the experience.

Evenings are spent laughing together as you recount the day's events around a barbeque, with today's catch the star attraction.

Layer upon layer of moments are etched ever deeper into your relationship with a place. Eventually, it becomes a part of who you are. A lucky charm, a world to escape to, a welcoming friend, a tranquil retreat when the rest of your life becomes too intense. It's simple. It demands nothing of you but your presence.

It's home. It's where your heart is. This is your happy place.

THE SEAWEED PICKERS

ROBIN COLLINS —

TAUROA POINT, NORTHLAND

'This is the snapper hole,' Robin tells me with a big smile on his face, revealing a lifetime of memories spent here on the edge of a rock that leads to a deep blue abyss.

'That rock we passed on the way in — that's mussel rock. You can get big green-lipped mussels there. And up that river is the watercress and where we get pigs.'

He surveys the beachscape like a king might look upon his kingdom. It's fitting. At 75, Robin has spent his whole life here, as did his parents before that. He's a second-generation seaweed picker.

Life at the end of Tauroa Point, which lies west of Ahipara, in Northland, has always been about resourcefulness. That's partly why Robin's tour feels more like I'm looking into his pantry and refrigerator than exploring the coastline.

'If you're not lazy up here, and you like

seafood, then you'll never starve,' Robin
chuckles. 'We get sea eggs and pāua and the
odd crayfish straight out the front of my place.
And we used to sneak into the rookery and
steal seagull eggs when we were younger. But
we're not allowed to do that now. They lay
three eggs — one each week — so we knew if
we took the first and second one, they were
fresh. If there were three, then we left them.'

He also dined on kererū when they were
on the miro berries, and toheroa, which were
plentiful along the sandy stretches to the
south.

Back at his freshly painted green hut,
Robin tells me he's the old kaumātua around
here — the elder. And he takes a dim view of
the pāua poachers who frequent the coast.

'You're allowed to take ten pāua a day and
sea eggs, well, I think you're allowed 50,' he
says. 'The Māori love them. I have to admit, I
like them, too.

'But when you've had a big feed of sea eggs,
mate, you don't want to fart in the house if
you have visitors.' He breaks into a hearty
laugh and rocks forward. 'That's the worst
thing you can do — you'll clear the whole
house. They just take off out both doors.'

When Robin retired, he decided to take
the bach on as a project. It had fallen into
disrepair with holes everywhere and rusted
iron — a far cry from the home his parents
built and that he grew up in.

'It was head down and arse up, and I got
into it,' he laughs.

PREVIOUS SPREAD
Robin's modest
bach is undergoing a
refurbishment.

ABOVE
Robin eats a stew dinner
that one of his four
daughters packed for
him.

OPPOSITE
Robin's kitchen.

As a kid, Robin would
wash in the bath
wedged into the drain.

Robin hopes the
younger generation will
follow his passion for
this coastline.

He added the deck, reclad the outside, renewed parts of the roof, then refloored, insulated and lined it. Over the next few days, he's planning to lay the new floor in the kitchen. He's hoping one of his four daughters will make curtains for the bach.

Robin says that people often don't believe he's 75.

'They can't get over how, at my age, I come out here and hand-dig all these drains, rip the bach down and put it up myself, do all the lining — do everything all myself,' he offers with a shake of his head. 'When you want relations to come out and help you, well, they all sort of disappear into the wild blue yonder.

'I'm just doing it up for the family, basically,' he says. 'Once I'm gone, it's up to them to keep it up to scratch, and I think they will. They've seen all the effort I've put into it. I've done a lot of work here. They all know the story.'

He concedes that he was a 'stubborn old bastard' when it came to working on the bach.

'My girls are saying, "Dad! That's too much hard work." But I had the time. That was the thing, I had the time. So what's the mad rush? And it's enjoyable.'

Each piece of building material is brought in from Kaitāia, 17 kilometres away. Seven of those are on the sand and rocky beach, which is only passable at low tide.

Robin's home is in Kaitāia — up on a hill with sea views. In his garage is a big SUV, and a Senator boat that he bought new last year sits next to it. Both hardly get used.

'I'd rather come out here,' he grins.

To get to the hut, he has an old Mitsubishi Challenger 4WD that he's under-sprayed to prevent rust. Having been raised here as a kid, Robin knows that everything rusts on the edge of the Tasman Sea.

He tells me how they used to walk from the hut into Ahipara to attend school every day.

Then, along with his brother and sister, they'd walk back again.

'In those days, there was no such thing as shoes,' he smiles, shaking his head. 'We had bare feet. We were tough as. We were tough and we were fit. If it rained, well, you were in the shit.'

He can still remember his first pair of shoes.

'They were sand shoes and I actually refused to wear them for one reason: I was scared they might wear out too quick! I saved them and just wore them for special occasions, but in the end I couldn't help it. It wasn't long before they fell apart.'

His parents eventually bought a couple of horses for the kids to ride to school.

'In those days, that was what happened,' Robin says. 'You had all the kids at school with horses, all tied up within the property. Those horses got cunning, though. We let them go in the paddock at home and they knew after a while that they were going to have to carry these bloody kids to school. We'd try to catch them and they'd run away — you couldn't get near them. So we got even more cunning. When we did finally get hold of them, we tied long ropes around their necks and let them go in the paddock. When we went up to get them to go to school, we'd just grab the rope. They were hard days, but they were good.'

He says they ate red meat probably once a fortnight back then. Relations in town would

ABOVE
Robin and his dog Possum walk out on the reef he grew up on.

NEXT SPREAD
The huts at dusk.

bring out mutton and exchange it for pāua and crayfish. Crayfish could be caught in the rock pools in front of the hut and pāua was everywhere. Any time the farmer up the back killed a beast, he'd drop some meat down to them.

'We had no power — no fridges, nothing,' Robin recalls. 'But we had a big outdoor safe. It had all this very fine mesh in it. You'd open it up, put all your meat in there, hanging up, shut it up so the flies couldn't get to it. It was surprising how long that meat lasted — the sun would semi-dry it.

'We were pretty basic. We ate a lot of seafood, fish, shellfish and stuff like that. It wasn't a flash diet, but it was a healthy diet. Mum had a big vegetable garden. She grew everything, including lots of kūmara.'

Like the other 15 or so families living here in the 1950s, Robin's parents picked agar seaweed for a living.

'Back in those days, you never got the benefit,' Robin explains. 'You just had to get out there and work your arse off to get what you wanted.'

Two species of agar seaweed were identified in New Zealand when the Japanese supply was threatened during World War Two. The agar was used to make sea-milk custard, for growing bacterial cultures, and used in medicines and foods.

'We'd pick the seaweed at low tide,' Robin explains. 'You'd get out in the water and pluck big bunches of seaweed, and carry it

up in sacks — it was hard work. And then the
next step was to clean it and get all the shell
and stuff off it. And then you'd lay it out on
the paddocks and dry it. Once it became dry,
you'd bundle it up and store it in a shed until
you were ready to bale it — like baling sheep
wool, but we didn't have a press. Our press
was our feet — we'd jump all over it and ram
some more in.'

When the families had 20 or 30 bales,
they'd call in Kaitāia Transport. They'd take it
through to Wellington, where the government
collected and paid for it. That happened right
up until 2019, when the agar was mostly
replaced by synthetics.

'It's a shame because this guy just along
here, Frankie, he's got about ten or eleven
bales in his shed that he can't sell now. You're
looking at around $400 or $450 a bale — and
he's got eleven of them over there he can't get
rid of.'

Robin tells me that there were also times
when the seaweed didn't come in because of
weather conditions. That meant no income
for the families so, instead, they would go into
the Ahipara gumfields to collect kauri gum, or
kāpia. Kauri gum had been a big industry in
the mid- to late 1800s, but by the 1950s it was
winding up. The gum was used for making
varnish and mostly exported to Britain and
America.

'We all had baches up among the tea tree
on the gumfields. They were very basic. My
family used to collect big bags of this gum, sew
the tops and put them on an old sledge. They
had these draught horses; everybody put all
their gum on the sledge and we'd take them
down the old gravel road, drag them down
into Shipwreck Bay.'

In Shipwreck Bay, they'd meet the
PS *Favourite*, which would come up from
Auckland through the Manukau Heads.

ABOVE
The white sandy strip meanders past other huts, caravans and shacks as it turns south to the empty beaches beyond Tauroa Point.

OPPOSITE
Overgrown and forgotten. The end of the line.

NEXT SPREAD
Robin and Possum pause to observe the wild horses that also find contentedness in the coast of Tauroa Point.

They'd load the gum and ship it to Auckland, at least until April 1870, when a large south-southwest storm blew up and damaged the paddle steamer. Captain Dyason was forced to beach the vessel in the storm, saving his crew but destroying the boat. To this day, there is still a piece of steel from the wreckage poking up in Shipwreck Bay.

Like the weathered wreck, the huts have followed a similar course over the years. Most of the dwellings along the beach strip are falling apart, dissolved back into the swamp, lying crippled, or nothing more than a patch of scorched earth beneath a jumble of rusty roofing iron.

Robin says there are only two or three families here now: Frankie and a couple of others over a bit further. The point fills with about 70 people over the summer months.

The legal standing of the huts is nebulous. Tauroa Point is mostly managed by the local iwi, Te Rarawa. They erected two pou, warning posts, near the baches to help protect the fishery, a response to people taking too much. They also closed the road to protect the ageing community during New Zealand's April 2020 Covid-19 lockdown.

'For families that have lived out here, on the land here, we look at this as our land,' Robin explains. 'Nobody else dare come here to change that.

'It's the same as the guys along here,' he says, waving his arm along the coast. 'Where their bach lies, they don't own the land, just

like me. But that's their land — anybody who comes along there to try to claim it, well, get out.'

—

Nearly 100 metres south of the Collins' bach, Robin introduces me to Frank (aka Frankie) and Cath, who live here full-time. Frank's 63 and it was his grandmother who built the original hut. It now features in a painting that has made its way onto a collection of table coasters.

Frank's sister, Phyliss, and her husband, Conrad, are out to visit, but Frank takes time to prepare a rollie and show me around the place his mother grew up in and where he has spent his life, too. He's in no hurry.

The pace of life is slow, considered. Frank's work around the bach is well-intentioned, and by seaweed pickers' standards it's an enviable dwelling.

His lawn is green and the channels that drain the section are clear — some even grow watercress. Others draw into his drinking-water system. He shows me a vegetable garden that glows green with life. He stabs out a few weeds while we talk.

Frank's world might be slow, but I can see how busy he is. The bach has had an extension from when he was a boy, and he's plumbed in a new gas hot-water shower. Like Robin's bach, his 12-volt electricity comes from a solar panel set-up he's put together. He tells me he has plans to go further with solar, as he tests his bank of batteries — confirming a good charge with his broad grin.

The inside of the bach is small but purposeful. The water runs clear from the tap and he's hoping to attach a 12-volt fridge to the solar circuit. The goal is to keep his running costs as low as possible. His outgoings

ABOVE
Frank's grandmother built this bach. He and his mother both grew up here.

OPPOSITE
(Clockwise from left)
A diver returns on dusk with a harvest of pāua and kina.

Frank holds up a frond of agar seaweed that, until 2019, was his source of income.

Once the agar was replaced with synthetics, Frank ended up stuck with nearly a dozen bales of seaweed that should have been worth around $450 each.

The rich peat soils grow incredible crops.

Frank's sister Phyliss shares a painting of the original hut.

are minimal: food, Ranfurly beer (the cheapest at his local PAK'nSAVE) and gas for the hot water. But he's not content with the $100 it costs him to refill his gas bottle, when it lasts only three months.

'I can improve on that,' he says, admitting that the hot shower had been welcomed by Cath. 'She feels the cold in winter.'

—

I follow a group of six wild horses back along the beach to Robin's hut. He's inside reading a book. Possum, his beloved dog, raises the alarm as I approach. I can see a lot of books are getting read in between his laying of the new floor.

'I have to admit, I like to get away from town,' he tells me as we sit on the deck in the afternoon sun. 'I just like to get away every now and again. I like to have my own space, if you know what I mean? Don't get me wrong — I love the missus and all that, but she's just like, "Pack your gear and go!" She's good, eh?'

The tide is nearly full and the water washes the vehicle tracks smooth in front of the hut. It's incredibly close and Robin tells me it sometimes spills over onto the edge of his lawn.

'It never comes up under the bach. By the time it does, I will have carked it anyway, so I don't care,' and he erupts into a fit of laughter. 'That will be the family's problem then.'

THE PADDLERS OF TE TII

DANNY AND TUPPY KAIAWE —

TE TII, BAY OF ISLANDS

'The waka is the vehicle for bringing people together,' Danny Kaiawe tells me in the early morning mist at Tapuaetahi Beach.

We're standing looking north from the grainy sands as teams prepare themselves for the seventh edition of the Pearl of the North waka ama competition. A low, rolling swell breathes in and out of the bay. Danny, 61, appears content.

'The waka reflects the people in it,' he continues. 'If it runs rough, then there's a mental issue within the team — it's not together. They're not smooth. When you sort that out, then the waka will run smooth. That's how we teach the boys — the young people who have all learnt right here.'

Danny and his wife, Tuppy, take in kids who have experienced hardship in their homes and lives. They put them into the waka

in front of their house in Te Puna Inlet, at Te Tii, alongside Whitiora Marae. There they tell them to forget what's around them, to focus on the paddle action and the horizon. In doing that, they give them direction — a purpose. It's a metaphor for life.

'It's the lifestyle they've come from — the cycle just repeats,' explains Tuppy, with a shake of her head. 'They are angry, angry children as a result of their lifestyle. And they realise that isn't normal. They come to us and they're eff this and eff that — it is just a second word to them in every conversation. We tell them if you want to be with us, then these are our rules: we don't want to hear you swearing and we want you to have respect for each other.'

She says that at times even brothers and siblings could not get on.

'Then we delve into why they are that way and to them that is normal — they never knew any different,' explains Tuppy. 'To learn about them you have to stand back and watch the dynamics and understand. It is like *Once Were Warriors* — you are on the outside looking in and you don't believe half the things that go on. It divulges itself as time goes on. We learnt to be hard-skinned about it. Just get on with it and not to take it all on, otherwise you'll get loaded — loaded with all their problems and everyone else's.

'That is the relief. That's when these boys start to realise that it is only them who can make it happen,' she smiles. 'They realise it is

PREVIOUS SPREAD
The fleet of waka ama paddlers stretches out from Tapuaetahi Bay.

ABOVE
Tuppy, Posh and Danny at home in their lounge overlooking Te Puna Inlet.

OPPOSITE
A post-race beach party seen from Danny and Tuppy's house.

NEXT SPREAD
Pōwhiri at Whitiora Marae, Te Tii.

up to them to do everything that they want to do . . . and to be good at it.'

Danny and Tuppy taught them how to train hard by setting that example.

'And that was our thing for them — if you want to get anywhere in life, you have to work hard. But you've also gotta be nice; not want to punch each other up, because that is their first reaction — to fight first. It is a struggle, a lot of struggle in their past, and it isn't their fault.'

I watch as the mist clears and pōhutukawa silhouettes on the near point appear to stretch out towards the sun's first rays. Danny and Tuppy offer a short, warm embrace with nearly every person who arrives. Others dart around in haste, and within the first hour the beach looks like a venue — the sand dunes lined with brightly coloured waka.

Danny was born in Kawakawa in 1959 and brought up at Te Tii. He is the second youngest in the family, one of 24 kids.

'Two families, one dad — he was a legend,' Danny laughs. 'There were no TVs back in those days. He was an incredible person. We used to go on these journeys every Sunday and people pulled off the dusty roads when he came along. I didn't realise at the time that he was actually the preacher.'

In 1974, Danny left Te Tii School and took up a scholarship at Hato Petera College on Auckland's North Shore.

'I didn't understand that it was only a two-year scholarship and so I went to Ōtāhuhu College for another three years,' he says. 'That changed my direction. I'm not Catholic, but Hato Petera was a Catholic school. So, I moved to a mainstream co-ed school, which was really an eye-opener compared to a Māori school. It was a cultural shock for me.'

His love for rugby bridged the gap for him. Danny was a halfback, a terrier of a player.

'I liked to put a bit of shit in, even on the locks,' he smiles, fond memories clearly flashing through his mind. '"Hit and run" was my motto. I played against all the All Blacks of that time. I got rucked over a beauty after a head-high tackle on Zinzan Brooke, and then "boomph", they all came over the top and blew me out of the ruck.'

When Danny's cousin moved into town and started a bar, he offered to sponsor Danny at 'whatever he wanted to do'.

'We organised rugby tournaments. It was a Sunday off — have fun and then have a drink,' he recalls. 'That was the culture. Everything was about the drink at the end of it.'

Tuppy and Danny have always been involved in organising sports, from their time with Mount Wellington Rugby to the bar in Ōtāhuhu.

'We thought we should start a team up — play rugby league and rugby,' Danny explains. 'And then we had a bit of a meeting and the name Coneheads came up. It was quite funny, so we agreed on that.'

The Coneheads team has been going now for 22 years.

'We've gone back a couple of times and we're not part of that scene anymore, but the boys introduce us as the original founders of the Coneheads.'

After school, Danny became a linesman for Mercury Energy and Vector, where he worked until 2010.

'I was living the life that everybody does in Auckland: hard and fast, drink and work,' he says. 'It came to a head when I had a blood test at work and the results showed that I had damage to my liver. I didn't take that too seriously until a few years later. I got a biopsy and realised that if I don't look after myself, then I would be facing health issues.'

Not long after, in 1999, Danny 'was tricked'

into taking up waka ama.

'My cousin who was running the bar, he said, "Bro, you'll love that sport. It will suit you." So I got into it and thought, *Shit, I love this sport.* I was sixteen stone and I went down to eleven or ten stone. Then the fulla who got me into it took off. He said, "See, I knew you'd like it." Ten years later, he told me, "I think I've created a beast." Well, he created more than that — I actually found my calling in it.'

Word of what Danny and Tuppy were doing for disaffected youth soon spread. Before long, they found themselves with kids from as far away as Wellington, Tokoroa, Hokianga — and, at times, whole teams of them. Logistically, it stretched them, but they persevered.

'I remember travelling in my blue truck,' Tuppy recalls. 'They'd jump in the back and were all squashed up — we had eight kids in there one time. That's how we travelled around. It was illegal, but the parents didn't have vehicles or couldn't afford to follow us with their kids. We'd tow the waka around with us. It was a buzz in itself — it wasn't the right thing to be doing, but when it's for something that's going to help the community, well, we had no choice.'

The Kaihoe o Ngati Rehia waka ama club is positioned perfectly in Te Tai Tokerau, Northland. The main centres for other paddlers are Whangārei, one hour south, and Kaitāia, one hour north. The club has access to three training environments: Lake Manuwai,

ABOVE
Race start at the seventh edition of the Pearl of the North.

OPPOSITE
(Clockwise from left)
Paddlers round Puketapu Rock.

A team slices through the bay.

Teamwork is vital.

Danny finds a seat as a steerer.

Te Puna Inlet and the ocean side of Purerua Peninsula.

Many attribute Danny and Tuppy's success to simply providing a strong male role model in the lives of these kids. Danny scoffs at that.

'Tuppy is the disciplinary person and I'm the nice one,' he smiles. 'Some people run and hide when she comes.'

Tuppy nods her head with a smirk, 'That is correct. I can't argue there.'

Born in Murupara, Tuppy is proudly 'from the bush'. Her upbringing was tough. Her mother passed away when she was just five.

'Me and my siblings, we were raised by our grandmother. Everything was simple — a simple lifestyle. We had a dirt floor and an open fireplace. You had to do everything

yourself, as little as you were. At five, six years old, you were sweeping floors, doing dishes, helping with the bread, chopping wood, feeding the animals — as you do out in the country. I grew up a worker and I still am.'

Tuppy doesn't remember her mother but is told she looks like her. She often wonders what would have happened if she was still here.

'It's just one of those moments you have. But I am so grateful for our grandmother and grand-uncle and our uncle who raised us. Their values I always hold close to my heart.'

Tuppy also had many siblings, including a sister who died at birth and a brother who was killed in the forestry service.

'I had a second brother who was adopted

out because a cousin couldn't have a baby. And then my mum and dad fostered a girl. Then I came along and they fostered a boy after me. But then my mum passed.'

Tuppy now has a daughter living in Rotorua and a son in Christchurch.

With the fighting spirit engrained in her early life, it is no surprise that she and Danny hit it off when they met at a rugby function in the Bay of Plenty.

When Tuppy joined the Northland waka ama team, she was 'just the newbie'.

'But you catch on fast, and you gotta work it out or you get kicked off the waka,' she laughs. 'They don't muck around in that sense, and I like that kind of attitude. That was me, too. I knew I had to shape up or ship out.'

From the time Tuppy joined the new team, she was winning age-group medals at every nationals held after that. In 2018, she travelled to Tahiti to compete in the World Championships, where she won triple gold in the W12 500, the W6 500 and the W6 1000 categories.

'Triple gold had never been done in those age groups. We broke a couple of world records.'

Danny leans in to admit that he was going to do the same at the 2020 World Championships in Hawai'i, but they were cancelled because of Covid.

—

Back at their home perched above the inlet, Danny has planted a tropical oasis that references Tahiti, Rarotonga and Hawai'i — the places that he has travelled to with waka ama.

'I came home and I realised I didn't need to go anywhere. It was all here for me. And I

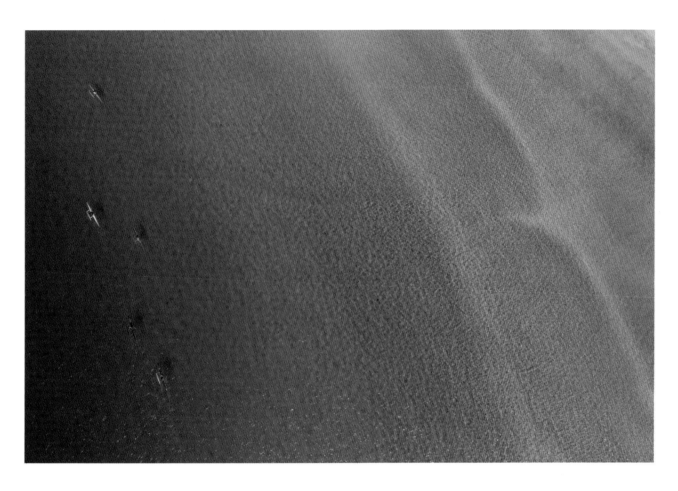

ABOVE
Paddlers carve through
the crystal water of
Tapuaetahi Bay.

OPPOSITE
Danny's niece Trisha
Kaiawe, with partner
Mokai and their sons
Samuel, four, and
Thomas, one, at the waka
ama-inspired mural on
the road to Te Tii.

Te Tii was known as
Bagtown many years
ago when a lot of homes
used hessian sacks for
wall linings instead of gib.
One of the first teams
was called the Bagtown
Boys as a result.

The Ngunguru team pulls
to the finish line.

NEXT SPREAD
Colourful waka at
Tapuaetahi.

want my friends to be here with me. At some
point, I was asking myself, *What would my
father wish me to do?* He was a preacher and
I didn't want to be a preacher. What was
his kaupapa about? His kaupapa was about
people. I probably turned it around to suit,
but I still think it's all about people. We did
that through sharing our love of the waka. All
the people here are a result of that over time. I
finally got them up here. That was my dream.'

The seed for the Pearl of the North event
took root when Danny ventured over the hill
to Tapuaetahi with his Tahitian friend, Jean
Tetohu, many years earlier.

'I said, "Bro, what do you think?" He said,
"Mate, you got it here." You know what I
want? I want the Tahitians to be racing here —

the best in the world. I think I'm getting close to that,' Danny turns to me with tears welling in his eyes.

'I'm proud of my family. We tried to create something for the whole community. Not just us, but to get the community involved.'

Danny says the racing takes care of itself, but the food is the most important part of the gathering. All the food is harvested locally including kina, oysters, smoked mullet and snapper. Danny often puts nets out himself.

'One time, I put the net out and then we had waka training with some young girls,' he smiles. 'I said, "Okay, let's go and pick up our net," and it was full. A stingray was flapping in the net and the crew of girls were screaming. We pulled it in and it was high tide, and we all cleaned up the fish. They hadn't done that before. What an experience. I like those random moments. They were buzzing, we all were.'

When it came to people power, Danny told me that's where the Te Tii community shone.

'It's like the waka philosophy — everybody pulling in the same direction at the same time. Same pressure, everything the same. If you have different factions or pressure, or whatever, it's going to be wobbly. The waka analogy is something they can keep with them for life.'

Tuppy smiles and nods her head in agreement.

'Everything has its ups and its downs, no matter what you do,' she offers. 'You can have

ABOVE
Danny shares a laugh with the crew as they prepare seafood.

OPPOSITE
Many hands make light work . . . and for a lot of laughter.

Danny explains the course to participants.

Post-race, unwinding in front of Danny and Tuppy's home.

NEXT SPREAD
Te Tii juts out into Te Puna Inlet.

a good day at training and then a shocking day — it's never the same.'

When Danny and Tuppy first came home to Te Tii, the club had no money. Kaihoe o Ngati Rehia Trust was brand new. They survived by collecting oysters and selling them to raise funds for the club so they could take the kids to the nationals. They earned quite a reputation. The club's first World Championship team was called the Fat Oysters.

One year, they took the Fat Oysters team over to the World Championships in Australia.

'We had it written on the back of our car: *Fat Oysters*,' Tuppy recalls. 'People followed us to the venue and came up to us: "Hi, we'll buy some!" We said, "Buy some what?" They said, "Some fat oysters!" We told them that was actually our team name. It was very funny.'

—

Race day is a swirl of colour and warm-hearted competition. Tupuria King emerges the victor — a humble, powerful, positive athlete. He sits down with about 400 others for a feast of seafood and hāngi at Whitiora Marae. It's a fever pitch of bench-racing, what-ifs and accounts of the drama that unfolded earlier in the day.

'Winning a race — being the best paddler out there — it's not really what the Pearl of the North is,' says Danny as he surveys the gathered paddlers and support crews. 'It's not about that at all. It's about everyone being on the same plateau. They could be in front of us, but we come with the feeling that: wow, this is so awesome. It's not about thrashing everybody, or coming last. They enjoy the race and experience some beautiful things along the way. Or, in this case, everybody walked away from the event rubbing their pukus because they had overeaten,' he laughs.

For one night of the year, Danny and Tuppy allow a few drinks on the beach in front of their waka ama garage. The paddlers and crew staying at the marae wander down to take in some songs by local band, Pearl Jam. The evening is filled with laughter and song.

—

Exhausted after a huge clean-up session at the marae, I sit down on the deck of Danny and Tuppy's home, which they built in 2010. They tell me that a lifetime supply of oysters secured all the aluminium joinery and windows, thanks to their friend, Anthony Cribb, who lives in Tauranga.

'He made two trips to Tauranga in one day to deliver it all,' he shakes his head.

Their dog Posh drifts around us as we talk. I ask Danny and Tuppy what they dream for the future.

'You saw it yesterday,' Danny smiles. 'It has already come to fruition. It's happening. But including this village coming on board. The smoking and the drugs, the P, they aren't helping anyone.'

Tuppy tells me the drugs right here in Te Tii, like many places in New Zealand, are very bad.

'About six months ago, we had a shooting.' She waves her arm across the ridge. 'Just over here. It doesn't matter where you are in New Zealand, it is everywhere. Here, in this village, we are all family, so it frustrates me. But they've got to find that stop button. No matter what you say and do, they've got to have that stop button for themselves.'

'We want the village to come on this ride with us on the waka,' offers Danny. 'It's going the healthy way.'

THE ECO DREAM

MALCOLM AND MELANIE RANDS

— MAMAKI, MATAPŌURI BAY

We climb a ridge using a seldom-used trail.
It weaves through mature natives. It's hot and
we're puffing. The summit of Matanui, clad
in trees, is somewhere beyond the canopy.
Malcolm Rands pauses to describe the genesis
for the idea he had more than 30 years ago:
to build an ecovillage. It's a simple, beautiful
dream.

Malcolm wanted the rain that fell
on Matanui to quench the canopy, the
understorey and the forest floor. He envisaged
it filling the streams, the ponds, dams and
reservoirs, and running through the homes in
the village and back into Te Wairoa Stream,
unsullied from its journey. From there, it
would continue its path as it wound its way
through the valley floor to meet the Pacific
Ocean at the southern end of Matapōuri Bay.

The vision was as idealistic as it was idyllic.
But Malcolm was determined.

'In the summer of 1984, I walked with some friends along a farm track four kilometres inland from the Northland coast,' he recalls. 'Into this valley, with hillsides covered in grass and tea tree. About 60 acres of the 150-acre property was covered in quite mature native forest, but the rest had been cleared many years before by fire and, like much of the farmland in Te Tai Tokerau, Northland, had been planted with drought-loving kikuyu grass.

'On the walk, we noticed small streams coming down from the neighbouring forest reserve and feeding into Te Wairoa Stream. Having already spent a few years looking for a place to create a community together, we knew that we'd found what we'd been looking for. Our home, our tūrangawaewae.'

Two years later, in 1986, they bought the property. Malcolm and Melanie, his wife, moved onto the land with two other families.

'We had the idea that, by combining resources, it would be possible to create a living environment more physically and socially satisfying than usually available through individual ownership,' Malcolm explains.

Mamaki is owned by a trust. Partners do not own a freehold piece of land, but are granted a licence to occupy their site by the trustees. And there are provisions for a partner to be able to on-sell to a new partner. That has happened only once in 35 years.

To begin with, they camped in the valley in tents and caravans throughout summer

and rented a cheap bach in Matapōuri Bay for winter.

'There was no proper access road and no electricity back then, so winters at the beach were a restful break.'

And still to this day, the white sands of Matapōuri Bay play a part in the Mamaki story. The beach curves for almost a kilometre between the rocky headlands standing sentinel at each end. A favourite fishing spot can be found on the northern headland, near where a large rock pool forms the mermaid pool, Te Wai o Te Taniwha.

'We mainly caught kahawai, but also the occasional snapper or kingy. But that has changed with a rāhui now in place.'

Ngātiwai members of Rangiwhakaahu Marae at Matapōuri took matters into their own hands in April 2019 after the area became inundated with tourists, which resulted in pollution from sunscreen chemicals, urine, rubbish and other damage. Malcolm and Melanie fully support the rāhui.

'It highlights the importance of guardianship and issues around over-loving and over-exploiting something,' says Malcolm. 'The rāhui was such a positive thing and it wouldn't have happened without the local iwi. They just said, "Bugger it, let's just do it." Then the council and everyone else followed them. They're Ngātiwai — people of the sea. They are a coastal iwi stretching along our coast, to Great Barrier Island and over to the Coromandel.'

The rāhui has changed the fishing grounds, but quality of life is bountiful in Mamaki. Forests, gardens, chickens and goats provide food in abundance — the valley is thriving.

'We try to approach land management matters using the principles of organics, permaculture and sustainability,' Malcolm says.

PREVIOUS SPREAD
The Tutukaka Coast is a natural extension of Mamaki. Malcolm and Melanie Rands enjoy the dusk at Sandy Bay.

OPPOSITE
Malcolm and Melanie designed their house around a principle of community.

ABOVE
Outdoor living in the ecovillage.

He says the average amount of time New Zealanders stayed on a piece of land was only seven years, which meant that not many people got to see what happens in the long term.

'I think that if we treated the land as if it was going to stay in the family and be passed on to our great-grandchildren, then we'd take better care of it,' he smiles.

Mamaki has six houses, built and established on the slopes of the hills to save the fertile flat land for crops, grazing and orchards. Families have created family hubs by adding tiny houses, which now equate to about 18 roofs that can be slept under.

'One of the important things we did in the village early on was to establish a legal structure to protect the land from speculative interest,' Malcolm explains as we make our way back to the valley below. 'The land is owned by a legal entity called the Te Wairoa Trust, and each of the partners leases a 2-acre section from the trust on which to build their house, plant trees and a garden.'

The radical thing Mamaki did was to cluster the houses instead of scattering them over the land to give their occupants privacy. That concept came from a 1977 book called *A Pattern Language* by Christopher Alexander, Sara Ishikawa and Murray Silverstein.

'Our houses at Mamaki are close enough that you have a bump space — you see your neighbours when you walk out of your house. The authors of *A Pattern Language* spent years

ABOVE
Visits to Whale Bay are cherished by the Rands family.

OPPOSITE
(Clockwise from left)
The stunning Whale Bay.

Ahi and her friend swim at Mermaid Pool before the rāhui came into place.

The Tutukaka Coast.

travelling around the world, going to every type of culture there was. And from that they determined what always works for humans and what doesn't.'

Malcolm tells me that 99 per cent of attempts at developing a sustainable eco-conscious community have failed.

'It's quite an idealistic thing to do,' he says. 'People go in with their friends and don't put any structure in. They think, *We're all good people*, but humans are humans and problems always come up. And then when they're at each other's throats, they try to put a structure together. But the trust has gone.

'We put massive energy into a structure and our way of working together — the legal side — at the very beginning of the first year. And that hasn't changed. It has been tested at times, hugely. And it's not as though we're all bliss here either, because we're humans. But because we had that structure, it has prevailed.'

And that has been reinforced with the next generation starting to move back to Mamaki.

'That's incredible, because that's where most of these things don't happen. They usually end up with a lot of geriatrics and then it folds,' Malcolm smiles. 'We've got six kids who've come back now and there's the next generation as well, with a baby living here with their parents and grandparents.'

Mamaki is not a commune and it is not

based on any religion. Residents can have as much or as little contact as they want with other partners.

'However, Mamaki seems to appeal to people who enjoy what we call "active neighbouring",' Malcolm says. 'Especially as that relates to making life easier around childcare, transport, property management and just having fun.'

—

The next day we walk to Whale Bay and it feels like an effortless connection, a coastal limb of Mamaki.

Malcolm and Melanie raised their two girls, Ahi and Keva, in this environment. Their backyard included streams, wetlands, a dam, kiwi and other native birds. They grew up in a country lifestyle that Malcolm describes as 'a great, natural and free-ranging environment for children and adults'.

As we head to the water's edge, they tell me 'Mamaki' is a Sanskrit word meaning 'spirit of the fertilising waters'. The name has proven to be very auspicious: many children have been born in the valley.

'When our daughters Ahilapalapa and Keva were born, we planted flowering trees on each of their whenua [placenta]. A beautiful ivory-coloured magnolia for Ahi, which flowers for her birthday in July, and a crepe myrtle for Keva, which blooms with bright pink flowers in early February.'

Ahi was born in 1987 and Keva in 1990. Mamaki had six households living in the village then — many with children of a similar age. When Keva was little, they had a tradition of celebrating her birthday every year with a picnic at Whale Bay.

'It's a magical place and we still love to cook dinner on the beach there at night,'

ABOVE
The Rands' house
nestled in the gardens of
Mamaki.

OPPOSITE
Malcolm in his happy
place.

Melanie is the quiet
achiever of the dynamic
duo.

It takes a special bond to
build an ecovillage.

Malcolm tells me. 'If we're lucky, we get to swim among the phosphorescence in the moonlight, winding our way back up the hill track afterwards, in the dark with our torches.'

—

Back in the village, Melanie sets an outdoor table as Malcolm shuffles steak around on a smoky barbeque. Two giant pūriri trees reach up in front of the house, providing shelter and food for kererū and tūī. Underneath them is a forest of young nīkau palms growing from seeds dropped there by the pigeons. The pūriri trees have always been very special to the Rands; 32 years ago, before the nīkau forest was there, Melanie and Malcolm were married beneath them.

The Rands' home was designed using ideas from *A Pattern Language* and features an open living space that includes the kitchen area and a large table, and a sleeping area where the beds are curtained off, each opening into a communal changing area.

'When the children were younger, it meant we were all closely connected to each other throughout the night and we could hear each other breathing.'

Malcolm and Melanie lived in the house for about three years before they got electricity. They had a wood-fired stove with a wetback, which they did all their cooking on. It heated all their hot water.

'Once a week, I made sourdough bread,' Malcolm recalls. 'I could make up to nine loaves in one day, with the kids playing around me, and I'd deliver them to people in the village. Often, they'd give me things in return, like fish or veges from the garden. It was hard work at times, but we loved it.'

Gardening organically, they were very confident in their ability to protect the streams from pollution. But they hadn't initially considered the water coming out of their houses, which also ended up in the waterways.

'When we looked at the chemicals used in our supermarket-bought cleaning products, shampoos and soaps, we were horrified,' Malcolm says. 'Some of the chemicals we were using inside our homes were actually worse than the ones we'd been so careful to avoid using in the garden.'

In their search to find ways to detox their home, they realised that other people ought to be doing the same. So they started to put together a business specialising in basic products like these.

'That was the birth of ecostore and it has been an incredible journey.'

When the first batch of ecostore products shipped out from the basement of the Rands' home in 1993, it was well ahead of its time. Consumers lapped it up and the business went on to become hugely successful. Malcolm and Melanie exited the business in 2015, but Malcolm stayed on for a few more years

ABOVE
The goats play their role in giving life to the Mamaki ethos.

OPPOSITE
More than 35 years later, the roots of Mamaki have a strong hold.

Chickens beneath the fruit trees in the village.

No dogs.

to help smooth the transition.

'I tell people I'm in my Colonel Sanders stage,' he laughs. 'And I don't even have to open any chicken restaurants, so I've got it sweet.'

Malcolm and Melanie have now moved back to Mamaki permanently, with Ahi and Keva joining them whenever they can.

'Life takes on a different rhythm here. We love waking up to the sounds of birdsong of the tūī and bellbirds, and going to sleep to the sounds of morepork and kiwi. We eat our meals outdoors and take in the spectacular stars at night, work in the garden and catch up with the other families for coffee or shared meals.'

They're far from retiring to the good life. They're still working on various projects, including Bucket, a direct, community-driven fundraising model.

'We're proposing to completely change the model of how online fundraising can work,' he explains. 'We're trying to make giving an easy habit with full transparency, where you know exactly where your money is going and you're actually creating community at the same time, with the people you give money to, and also other people in your group — all while supporting the things you believe in.'

Their second project is called Bumpspace, and it draws on their knowledge from living in an ecovillage for the past 35 years. It aims to bring the same concept into an urban environment and challenge the New Zealand convention of a 'single-storey pioneer cottage on its own land'.

'Suburbs are very isolated places — not many people know their neighbours. It destroys community. With Bumpspace, of course, it will be eco, with gardens and orchards as part of that. But, because of the design, it's going to be very hard to live

there without casually bumping into your neighbours in your everyday movements.'

Malcolm wants to see Bumpspace realise proof of life and plans to share the knowledge with others. Melanie stands right beside him.

—

Melanie was teaching in 1984, and could never have imagined then what lay ahead for her, or the different turns her life would take. She's achieved success in fine arts and creative writing, and has served on the board of Greenpeace Aotearoa for the past six years.

'Their work to protect our oceans is very close to my heart,' Melanie explains. 'Luckily, I'm comfortable wearing a lot of different hats and I'm a creative problem-solver, so I think Malcolm and I will continue to make life better and more interesting for each other — and hopefully for other people, too!'

Melanie smiles and tells me that one of their strengths as a couple is being values-driven.

'Even though it has been a challenging mix of hard work and sacrifice, our work together has always been bolstered by a belief in what we are doing. It has tested us to the max at times — we're both very determined people who can cause things to happen when we're in agreement. We've learnt to work through disagreements pretty quickly.'

Malcolm sits on the couch next to Melanie and tells me he is a very lucky person.

Matapōuri Bay plays a special part in the lives of the people of Mamaki.

'Often things turn up just when I need them, and often amazing people will just turn up and help me,' he says. 'I feel quite fated. I'm not really a solo artist — I've always been collaborative, even at ecostore. It's not been my journey alone. Having an amazing person like Melanie by my side has made the whole thing work. I couldn't have done it without her. When I look back, I'm really, really happy. I've got nothing left to prove.'

The village below the ridgeline.

THE HEALING WATERS OF PAREPAREA BAY

JAIMIE SCOTT AND KAREN

BLENNERHASSETT —

WHANANĀKI

We step on to the sand right where Karen and Jaimie first wheeled their caravan into position 27 years ago. Jaimie is 50 now, while Karen's age is 'classified'. She's older than him, but she has his measure in youthful vigour.

They're in their wetsuits, carrying surfboards and eagerly eyeing the swell as it rolls into the southernmost scallop of Pareparea Bay. Their paths first crossed when Jaimie and his brother worked at Kamo's Northland Sailboards, or NSB, the surf shop belonging to Karen and her partner, Boyd. That was before the unthinkable happened.

Boyd passed away after a battle with cancer. Not long after, Jaimie's brother was involved in a car crash.

'Jaimie and his brother were helping me sort everything out with the shop,' Karen recalls. 'Then Jaimie's brother became a quadriplegic.'

THE HEALING WATERS OF PAREPAREA BAY

'He lived for two weeks after the crash but he was just a head that could breathe. It was hard,' Jaimie shares, shaking his head at the thought.

Their future would be inextricably linked by their losses — the shared grief binding the two together.

'That was partly why we came out here,' Jaimie continues. 'We just wanted to hermit out and hide from the world.'

Jaimie and his brother were very close. They built surfboards together and he was Jaimie's surfing buddy. The experience changed Jaimie's outlook on life.

'I reckon seeing things like that helps you to always look at the positives — the negatives are too gnarly.'

It had a profound effect on Karen, too.

'When we had the surf shop in town, I also had an old folks' home,' she says. 'I saw that life was short. No one in there ever regretted not having things, but they regretted not doing things. I realised it was all about living your life.'

—

Jaimie was born in Australia. He grew up between the Gold Coast and the Sunshine Coast, learning to sail and surf along the coastline. At 12, he moved to Northland and started high school in Kerikeri, before his parents bought land and built a house at Sandy Bay. He moved to Whangārei Boys' High School, then pursued a sailmaking apprenticeship in Auckland.

'I was in Auckland when I got a call from my windsurfing sponsor, NSB. They asked if I wanted to come up and set up a windsurf sail loft. Because I was a passionate windsurfer, I was like, "Yeah, sweet." I was out of Auckland and back to my roots.'

Jaimie ran the sail operation and started making surfboards under the tutelage of Boyd. When tragedy struck, Jaimie and Karen

decided to shut the shop. They moved to the valley in 1994. They lived a simple life in the caravan down the front while building the Tribal Surfboards factory out of recycled material from the old shop.

'That was the best place to live,' Jaimie smiles. 'Stepping out right onto the sand was nice. There was no maintenance. It was the best place to rethink life and get back on track.'

Surfing was at a peak in the mid- to late 1990s and Tribal quickly gained a big chunk of the market in the north for performance short boards.

'We had maybe seventy per cent of the market,' Jaimie says. 'It was good — it seemed like everyone was getting boards off us. We were doing up to five boards a week.'

When Karen fell pregnant with their daughter Billie in 2000, they decided it was time to build the main house.

'We thought we should do it now or we probably won't do it,' laughs Jaimie, as he thinks back to their incredible ambition. They had been largely encouraged by the promising surf business and the fact they could run the business from where they lived, with the factory on-site.

—

As a young surfer, Jaimie would buy his boards off local shaper Col McNeill, who shaped under the Hurley brand. He was part of the inspiration that led Jaimie into making boards.

Col succumbed to cancer around the same time as Boyd did. That had a profound effect on Jaimie.

'It was hard for me, knowing how toxic making surfboards was and knowing two mates who made boards and who had got cancer,' says Jaimie. 'That's why I pursued the designing — as soon as there were programmes to start doing that, and I didn't

PREVIOUS SPREAD
The home of Jaimie Scott and Karen Blennerhassett is nestled on the Whananāki coastline.

OPPOSITE
Extensive plantings and restoration have filled the private valley with birdlife.

Jaimie and Karen have created their perfect adventure lifestyle together.

have to be in the shaping bay, well, that was the direction I took.'

Their hand was forced when surfboard imports — cheap boards from China, mainly — destroyed the local market around 2013.

'The market just faded and we got burnt by people,' recalls Jaimie. 'We had done our clothing as well, and the surf shops held out on paying us. We asked ourselves, "Do we want this headache?" It was confusing, because we were passionate about surfing and it just wasn't coming back.'

Karen adds that it was through no fault of the surf shops themselves.

'Everyone's intentions were good. It's just the way the industry went.'

'We never built the second house intending

to rent it out,' Jaimie says. 'We were going to pump up the factory and do the whole surf industry thing as our main financial support. It soon became obvious that the surf industry wasn't something that we could rely on. I was burnt out and we needed a change of tack.'

To add an income stream they made the decision to rent their house out. Karen says the house was nearly 10 years old by then, so they 'weren't precious anymore'.

Their guests fell in love with the private valley, beach, bush and total relaxation that the property exudes. Demand grew. They've had Benedict Cumberbatch stay, friends of Kim Dotcom, Jane Campion, Saudi embassy people — an A-list guest list.

'Because it's so private, people can sneak in here and hide away,' Jaimie explains. 'You see people turn up here all white and pasty, stressed out and everything — even getting here has been a mission. Then ten days later, after chilling out here, they go home fit, brown and happy. It's quite cool watching that transition. Breathe a bit of Pareparea air and you'll be right.'

With the property values soaring along the coast and the rates 'getting quite crippling', renting out the property when it suited them helped — and justified the amount of time they spent in the garden and on maintenance. Their goal has remained unchanged.

'We didn't want to leave the valley to work,' Jaimie says. 'We wanted to work here. Everything we've created has been about

ABOVE
Jaimie surfs when the wind is offshore, and goes kiteboarding when the wind swings onshore.

OPPOSITE
Loaded up for the trek around the rocks.

Karen laying her board on edge.

Karen helps Jaimie launch his kite.

being able to stay here and work.'

With the board business unstable, the challenges came thick and fast. Jaimie pursued the design route, and it paid off in an unexpected way.

'I'm pretty stoked with where I've ended up,' he smiles. 'It was a bit of a fluke, how it all worked out. I ended up designing, and not really figuring out how it would happen, and then North came along.'

—

North is a global action sports brand that started out in sailing in 1957. It now has headquarters in Europe, hubs in the USA and Australia, and its product-development, marketing and brand-management team is based in New Zealand. But it was when North Kiteboarding's research and development lead, a windsurfer from Christchurch, stayed at Jaimie's house that the stars began to align.

'They were looking for someone who kited and who could design surfboards because they needed a designer for kitesurfing boards,' Jaimie explains. 'He came and stayed here and we made a good connection. Then he rang me up and said, "Oh, the next time Shippies is good, give me a yell and we'll come up. We'll catch up and have a chat." And then it just so happened that we got the hell swell at Shipwreck Bay. It was five metres and a perfect twenty-second period. I hadn't seen it like that for fifteen years. I'm like, "Hey Mike, are you keen?" So, he comes up with jet skis and my job interview was virtually, "Okay, how hardcore are you, bro?" Just getting towed into some crazy waves at Shippies.'

For the past three years, Jaimie has been working with North as a designer.

'I started with kite surfboards, then the foil surfboards, and then there's the foil stand-up paddleboards, and then the kite foil boards,' he tells me. 'It has been endless; all just design work and working with factories in China.

Last year, I was meant to go to Maui and hang out with the team riders and just work on refining their boards. Then I was possibly going to Mauritius for the season's product launch. It's a pretty cool job, but we got shut down by Covid-19, unfortunately.'

For Jaimie, the role was a perfect fit. He has endless board-shaping files from years of designing surfboards with the two leading pieces of software, AkuShaper and Shape3d. Combined with his experience with windsurfers, understanding of snowboards and the wide range of boards he rides, he was able to hit the ground running.

'Shape3d is a little bit more of an engineering-spec program,' he explains as he pulls up a surfboard file on the laptop left open on his dining table. 'It's a bit more technical and that's what we use for those technical shapes — a bit more detail than a surfboard.

'We do heaps of prototyping — we did eighty to a hundred surfboard prototypes in the first year,' he says. 'We just rode them, tested them and refined them. We prototype with the factory we do production with in China, as we iron out lots of things through that R&D process.'

North Kiteboarding is the second-biggest kiteboarding company in the world, they tell me — and aiming to be number one.

'It's cool to be able to do it from here,' he smiles, watching the wind pick up out on the bay. 'It means you can get your water time

ABOVE
Jaimie in his original
shaping bay, up in the
back garden.

OPPOSITE
(Clockwise from left)
Sanding discs on the
wall of the shaping bay.

A well-used spray gun.

Inspecting a new Tribal
board.

in, do all your work, and all in the same day. That's what it's all about — making toys and playing with them. Most Kiwis dream of doing that.'

We watch the wind lap the surface of the ocean. At 20 knots, we should see white-capping; it's also the magic number for some wing foils Jaimie and his colleagues from North hope to test out later today.

The test foil wings are cut and shaped out of foam or timber using a computer-controlled machine and then laminated or vacuum-bagged for testing. They use a benchmark design and make four or five different wings — incremental variations — and then Jaimie and his colleagues will take them into the bay and test them.

'I'm pushing to make the ultimate surf wing, a wing that feels like a proper surfboard — there's not one yet,' he concedes. 'We're not surfing with them yet. We're close, but I want to lay it over, crank it and bounce off the whitewash.'

The prototypes are first tested in the bay, away from prying eyes and in a very creative environment.

'We're trying to nut out what everything does with the shapes and curves. It really is interesting — a bit like designing planes that surf,' he chuckles at the simple analogy. 'I don't know where to look exactly yet, but I'm looking at birds' wings, fish and I'm also considering what fins on surfboards do. I've learnt a ton about what fins really do on a surfboard — not just what we think they do. It's a world of thickness versus length, aspect ratios, hydrodynamics — so many factors. At the moment, we've got a wing that we know works and it works really well; it's one of the market-leader wings. But from there, I'm trying to translate my feel into the shape — the same as I would do with a surfboard.'

Jaimie first described that 'translating' process as having started with designing sails — plotting curves to get aerofoils. I ask him if he's learning from the America's Cup designers.

'With the new foil boards, I took total inspiration from them, and I like the look of the reverse shear features on modern race boats. They're not like a surfboard. There's a lot in the water release features.'

He tells me that's why he hasn't completely stopped Tribal. He has more to give for surfing.

'I've got a completely new type of surfboard that I'm going to bring to the market one day,' he smiles, shaking his head. 'It's like nothing that anyone has ever seen. I've been playing around with it for a long time. It's about flex. It's more snowboard-like than anything. It's finless, but it will have more grip than a finned surfboard. It's bio-directional. I'm hoping to bring something new to surfboard technology. I know the mechanics work, but the construction — to get volume so you can paddle is the challenge.

'Surfboards are really cool, but I'm sure we can do more on a wave with a new board design.'

He looks out the window and makes the call to go out. The wind is nearly where he thinks it should be. We're scrambling like kids to get out there, and the toys are kites, foil boards and inflatable wings.

—

Later, over dinner, with heavy rain washing salt from the balconies and walls of the house, the phone rings. It's Billie. She rings daily from Hawai'i. There is an early season swell forecast for the North Shore and she's keen to go and have a look, maybe a surf. She's understandably nervous.

Billie started surfing out the front when she was four and surfed regularly until she was 12. She always surfed for fun and never really thought of it as a sport, other than the contests her dad competed in. That all changed one day.

'They were picking the surf team at high school. One of my mates was a teacher and he was like, "Billie Scott, you can surf, can't you? You're in the surf team." She wasn't a contest surfer or anything at that point. She agreed to go in the team. So, we just went hard out and got her up to spec for the National Surfing Scholastics contest. It just took off from there. She wanted to do every contest — we travelled the country up and down. We did years of it.'

In her last year in the Under-20s, Billie finished the Billabong Series at the top. Then she started stand-up paddleboarding (SUP) and went to El Salvador with the New Zealand SUP team.

'She's been surfing and SUPing in Hawai'i,' Jaimie says. 'She just wants to have a blast, do a year of competing to see if it's a cool dream or a bad dream. She's twenty-one and just finishing her science degree at the end of the year. She did two years at Waikato, then won a scholarship to go anywhere, and she picked Hawai'i.'

I can imagine Billie growing up here as a child, but the reality was even cooler. In part because her parents had a 'live life to the fullest' attitude and had recently discovered snowboarding.

They pulled Billie out of school when she was eight and she did correspondence so that they could snowboard without feeling guilty about the number of days she took off school.

OPPOSITE
Jaimie puts a foil surfboard through its paces.

A new wing foil design about to be tested.

The North test team spreads out on the front lawn.

NEXT SPREAD
Pareparea Bay makes an ideal test bed for North.

'That's how manic we were,' smiles Karen. 'We hated snowboarding weekends because it was too crowded.'

It took a leap of faith to put Billie's educational needs in their own hands.

'When we first started out, I really worried,' admits Karen. 'Like at nine o'clock, all the other kids are starting to learn; what are we going to do? We just learnt that you can surf when the surf is good and learn when the rain comes.'

'We did maths on the beach in the sand,' Jaimie recalls. 'She'd write stories up in a tree hut up in some pōhutukawa tree. It was a pretty cool life for a grommie.'

They taught her basic maths, English and science and 'hammered it in'.

'We did something right, because she's a straight-A student. She's still getting As and topping the uni now,' Karen says. 'She's in the top five per cent in the university in Hawai'i and that's one of the top universities.'

Jaimie tells me she's not naturally clever — she's just a really hard worker.

She's also born into a family that makes things happen. I point out to them that there is no snow near Whananāki.

'It takes seven hours to get to Ruapehu,' Jaimie tells me. 'We leave at two in the morning and drive straight up the mountain. We're usually shattered that night.'

They wait until the weather forecast is bang on with freshies and just go.

'It's the same as chasing waves, really,' Jaimie smiles.

Jaimie says snowboarding was good because they discovered it late, so it was like a fresh addiction.

Jaimie and Karen are inseparable. They do everything together and seem completely in tune. When they can, they travel to the northern hemisphere for snowboarding — chasing powder — or visit their favourite island in Fiji for kitesurfing. Beneath the rosy picture, they admit they both work very hard.

They once nearly gave in to temptation and sold it all when Hugo Boss's son flew in with a chopper and threatened to offer them 'mega millions of dollars' for the property.

'We were tempted, but luckily he didn't come back to us,' Karen recalls. 'That was lucky. We only flashed on it for a little while. At the time, we were over the gardening and we were over the work.'

Jaimie shakes his head. 'You go through phases in your life. And we just wanted an easy way out. We'd worked our arses off.'

He and Karen pause for a moment, and I can see they're relieved they held on.

'As far as you can throw a stone, you can catch a fish,' Jaimie says, looking towards the bay. 'Billie used to get pāua at low tide, without even getting wet. There's a pinnacle out where the bombie breaks, out on the end of the islands — that's the go-to spearfishing and live-baiting spot for kingies.

'One of my workers used to come from Sandy Bay on a boat,' Jaimie begins. 'He used to come here and work, but nine times out of ten, he'd get sidetracked and go fishing. I'd be working away and he wouldn't have turned up, and I'd see his little boat sitting out there.'

'I remember one day, we were waiting and waiting for him and he brings the boat into the beach and comes running up with this fish,' Karen recalls. 'Shouting, "I've got to weigh it in, I've got to weigh it in!" He wanted us to stop what we were doing and drive him and his fish in to get weighed.'

Jaimie said they often got mussels on the rocks and crayfish all the way out on the point filling the cracks along the reef.

'We want to retire here. That's the goal,' Jaimie says. 'We want to hand it on to our daughter. She loves it. She was born here.'

THE MILLARS OF MONKEY ROCK

THE MILLAR FAMILY — PIHA,

WEST AUCKLAND

'It's a bit rotten,' Portia, 11, tells me as she and her older sister, Leia, give me a tour of their beachfront home at North Piha.

The dwelling is a near-classic 1960s retro beach bach, with only its aluminium joinery hinting at something more modern. It's a charming throwback to the bach heyday in New Zealand. But that doesn't seem to appeal much to the next generation; Leia and Portia determined that the house was haunted when their parents Carolyn and Stu first bought it in 2017.

'You didn't see this house before it was redone. It had lino floors and beige, yellowy walls, and holes everywhere,' Leia, 13, explains. 'I think it's super-cool here, but it would be cooler to have a new house.'

A small trail leads from the front of the house and up and over sand dunes, through 100 metres of low scrub and dune grass to

the black sands of North Piha. Monkey Rock stands sentry to the well-worn link between the wild Tasman Sea and the girls' home.

'It's pretty much asbestos,' Carolyn declares with a laugh. 'That's why it's still here — it's so durable. We did replace the whole front. That was rotten and falling apart. And behind the walls it is probably rotten, but what we can't see doesn't hurt us. We just go with it.'

Carolyn Gundy is a celebrated local architect operating under her C—Architecture brand. She's carved a reputation for creating spaces that bring the environment in and people together. She likes a challenge.

Together with her husband Stu Millar, they bought a 'gottage' — a 45-square-metre garage cottage in the hills behind their bach. They bought it in the real estate peak of 2005 and it 'nearly killed them'.

'We had two children, and our bedroom was behind the kitchen with curtains separating it,' laughs Caro. 'These two shared a tiny bedroom. Leia was two and had to sleep in a top bunk.'

Caro couldn't help herself and designed a grand and beautiful building for the site. When she realised it was costing way too much, she went back to her draughting table.

'What we loved about the little bach was that we had this communication all the time,' Caro explains. 'And we wanted to maintain that. The new house was two levels: the upper level was a mezzanine that looked over the

PREVIOUS SPREAD
Leia and Portia in their
element in front of their
family home at Piha.

OPPOSITE
Right on the beachfront,
the house feels more
like a home than a bach,
despite its compact size.

RIGHT
Portia, 11, Caro, 46, Nico
(dog), Stu, 47, and Leia,
13, with some of their
favourite surfboards.

double-height living and dining. We always had a sense of connection between the two levels — you could just yell out and the kids could hear you even though we were the level above.'

They built it in 2011 and their friend called it 'The Jewel Box'. It had marine ply on the inside, was cedar-clad with massive windows and set on a 2300-square-metre sprawl of native bush. The home featured in international design magazines.

'It was only 130 square metres, but that was in line with my vision to keep things small and sustainable,' Caro says. 'That was the cool thing about it — it had this beautiful volume, and it had great light and that connection to the bush. We had this amazing nīkau grove right outside to the east. The sun would come in every morning and stream through the nīkau fronds into our house.'

'We'd put so much money into it and so much effort. It was our lifetime dream,' Stu adds. 'We didn't really have any plans to go anywhere else, but I knew that I needed to find something better, otherwise Carolyn wouldn't want to leave that place.'

And that's when the beachfront bach came up — a wreck of a place that begged to be bowled.

'It was exactly what I'd always wanted,' says Stu with a smile.

They sold their designer home and bought the bach in 2017. They rented it out for a period of time until they realised that they

OPPOSITE
High-tide access to the Piha Bar is never easy, but the Millar family seem to love a challenge.

ABOVE
(Clockwise from left)
At 13, Leia is completely comfortable in the water.

Portia has her sister in her sights.

Portia the moment she realises a big set is looming.

Leia makes her way down a wave into the cove at South Piha.

couldn't visit their beach house when guests were staying.

'As soon as they were gone, we'd come down here and hang out,' Stu tells me. 'We'd go for a surf and just hang out here in the evenings. It was pretty cool.'

The bach grew on them and instead of demoing it, they got to work, with the help of friends, and ripped the lino out, repaired water damage, removed rotten walls, reclad the front and pulled out the rusted flashings.

'When we first decided that we were going to tidy it up, we wondered just how much asbestos there was going to be,' Stu recalls. 'I remember Caro and I were sitting in this room on one of the shitty old beds — they'd left all the furniture here as well. The place

just stunk. We looked at each other and said, "What have we done?" Then we went, "Okay, let's just get going." And we started ripping up the carpets, ripping everything out and painting it.'

The pressure came on when they had to get everything tested for asbestos, including the lino. Caro said that if that had been asbestos it would have turned its removal into a $20,000 job. They got lucky.

'It has got a really good feel to it, and it's the cheapest kitchen we could find,' laughs Caro. 'We didn't know what we were eventually doing in terms of demoing it and starting again, so we didn't want to spend the money on the kitchen, but it works.'

We sit and chat at a dining table that's

built into a stairwell. It's a focal point. Out the window, the giant form of Monkey Rock sits a stone's throw to the north.

'Monkey Rock makes it. It has a real presence and gives the bach a kind of solidity,' says Caro.

'When we first bought it, we'd cook dinner and then we'd take our plates and we'd walk out there and go and sit up on Monkey Rock to have dinner,' recalls Stu. 'That was pretty neat.'

Most of the rocks in Piha are named after some animal they resemble. Monkey Rock, or Makimaki, has three faces, and from the north side it looks a bit like a monkey.

Stu tells me about an old photo he saw once with a high-tide storm surge swirling

ABOVE
Their trail leads straight from the outdoor shower on the edge of the bach to the beach.

A typically busy morning in the Millar household.

around Monkey Rock's base, no doubt an uncomfortable vision given the proximity of his bach.

'We used to come down here when I was seventeen, meet up and we'd surf right here,' Stu tells me. 'We actually used to leave our boards on Monkey Rock. At high tide, you'd get sets come through and get close to the front of the rock, so we put our boards up on the rocks so they wouldn't be washed away. And that's in my lifetime.'

—

Stu grew up in Clevedon, on a 10-acre lifestyle property. He then boarded at Auckland Grammar School until his family moved to Takapuna on the North Shore and he became a day student. That's also when his passion for surfing ignited.

'We used to get a bus from town on the weekends and head to Piha for a surf,' he recalls. 'We did that a few times before we were stopped and weren't allowed to do it anymore.'

Living on the North Shore exposed Stu to a large crew of surfers, and they'd regularly surf Piha or O'Neills Reef.

He finished study and travelled to the UK, working in London and spending some time in Costa Rica. In London, he got into finance and fund management and worked for J.P. Morgan.

When he returned to New Zealand, he lived in Auckland for a short time before making the move out to Piha.

'Some friends and I rented a house on Beach Valley Road,' he recalls. 'I remember the first night we were there, my friend had a big Chevy truck and pulled up at my place on Gillies Ave. We loaded the pool table on the back of the truck and out we came. We had our sleeping bags and a pool table. We'd play pool and sleep on the floor and that was us.'

One of Stu's friends was seeing one of

Caro's friends at the time. They belonged to the Karekare Surf Club and it was at one of the parties that Stu and Caro first met.

—

Caro describes herself as a 'Westie girl from way back', having grown up on Scenic Drive in the Waitākere Ranges. As soon as she could, she moved to Piha and flatted with her friends. She has lived there, for the most part, ever since.

Family holidays to Taupō Bay gave Caro her first taste of the surf lifestyle.

'My parents were both teachers, so summer, winter holidays, boom: we'd go up there for six weeks at a time,' she explains. 'We had a caravan site on the beachfront, a to-die-for kind of a location. We owned it with three families — all my cousins. That's how we grew up on the beach; surfing and loving that kind of lifestyle from very early on. I boogie-boarded and we had white polystyrene surfboards.'

When she was 16, a friend of the family came up with a proper surfboard and cemented her love for the sport.

'I can still remember it. I came in and everyone clapped on the beach. I was into it from then on.'

Piha enabled Caro to indulge in her passion, but it also turned out to be a good place to raise children.

'There was quite an influx of children, all at the same time,' she explains. 'There's a preschool just down the road and, through that, we met all the mums and all the other kids, so they all hung out together.'

The mums would walk with prams and a posse of kids grew up together. They're the same ones who still surf together now.

'That's been amazing. It's a really cool environment for children — they just go to the beach every day. That's what they've grown up with; they're on the beach playing with

sandcastles every day of their life. It's pretty lucky.'

—

We wander along the track to the beach as the sun begins its descent into the sea. Stu, Leia and Portia, together with their little dog Nico, are wrangling a washed-up log off the beach and into the dunes. The dune grass is rendered golden by the evening sun.

I can tell by the look on Caro's face that she's in her happy place.

She tells me that Covid has revealed just how small their home is, now that Stu, who normally works in the city, is working from home.

'My awesome home office set-up, which I've only just sorted, proved to be way too cosy with Stu here,' she laughs. 'He's way too loud and I couldn't get the creative flowing. He's on Zoom meetings and the phone a lot. So I moved out to the lounge.'

Caro's work is mostly in residential architecture with the occasional commercial project. She specialises in coastal environments and has a very grounded take on building people's dream homes.

'Building in this environment is my thing. It's where I get my passion and where I get most excited. Sharing the rollercoaster journey of a house build with a client is also so enjoyable and rewarding. I have a home under construction halfway up the hill at

OPPOSITE
Stu drops into a wave
at the Piha Bar as
Leia paddles over the
shoulder.

ABOVE
(Clockwise from left)
Stu offers some advice
before a heat at a surf
contest in Kaikōura.

Leia and Portia in the
board room — a shed at
the back of their bach.

Portia and her friend,
Lola Groube, check out
the heat winners at a
contest in Whangamatā.

the moment — it's for a beautiful family that
has lived out here forever. They've had some
extremely tough times in the past, so it's been
a challenging project that I've poured my
heart and soul into.'

She has another project in Ōpito Bay on the
Coromandel Peninsula. It's a beachfront build
for a family who have had a bach down there
for three generations.

'They're building it with that future
generation in mind. The concept of it is as
a hub for the family to come and be. That's
the kind of thing I love doing: having a really
good concept and creating something that is a
reflection of the family and who they are.'

She tells me her work is about appreciating
the environment, responding to a site and

getting the most out of the sun and the view.

After spending a summer surfing at a
friend's cabin on the beachfront at Tairua,
they realised that size wasn't important to the
way a house embraced its occupants.

'That's the crux of it, really — we had
such a good time in a small, compact, really
efficient, beautiful space,' she recalls. 'We
realised we didn't need the full monty. We
don't need the square metres. We just need
quality. I studied that, but to experience it was
really helpful. We needed quality, we needed
experiences and little intimate moments all
around the place, but we don't need massive.
It works on so many levels — it works on
cost, it works on sustainability, it works on
quality. That's where I am at and where I try

to steer my clients. It comes down to being able to create experiences within the spaces.'

They've certainly achieved that in the bach. It has a feeling of home. A feeling that it is of the people who occupy it.

'The heart of the home is that space where everybody comes together,' Caro says. 'The sun shines in and you've got those moments where people are enjoying themselves and connected to the environment. That's my biggest thing in architecture — capturing that appreciation and awareness of where you are and your sense of place. If I can achieve that, then for me that's being successful.'

They're unsure of what to ultimately do with the bach. They know the existing home won't cater for growing teenage girls forever.

'We want to be able to create some spaces where the kids can just go,' Stu explains. 'Part of the new plan has got a games room, board rooms, where we can have all the boards, table tennis table and a pool table. And the kids' bedrooms are down there as well. So they can just run that whole space. They can come in from the surf, shower and hang out. It would be pretty mint for them.'

—

The next morning, we head to South Piha where the swell is more manageable. Leia and Portia are excited to hit the water with Mum and Dad. Every surf session has an element of competition to it. Leia is one of New Zealand's top female surfers in her age bracket. Portia's hot on her heels.

As we crawl around the rocks at high tide, Stu tells me he is the chief investment officer for Smartshares. It manages KiwiSaver funds, workplace savings, a range of exchange trader funds and is owned by the NZX.

'I really enjoy it — you're really involved with global markets, what's happening in the world economies. I've lived through a few of these crises, even back to the dot-com bubble and the global financial crisis. It's very easy to get caught up in either the greed or the fear that you see in markets.

'Outside of just going surfing every day, I think it is probably the next best thing for me.'

Stu's relationship with surfing initially never involved competitive surfing. Instead, he and his friends spent their time travelling around the country looking for waves.

'We found lots of them. I've got heaps of secret spots and I won't tell anybody about them,' he smiles. 'We still surf those places with my friends. No one knows about them and some of those places aren't far from Auckland.'

Once he moved to Piha and joined the Karekare Boardriders Club, he started to compete, including in a couple of nationals. He even made it to the finals once, alongside one of New Zealand's greatest: Maz Quinn.

'I remember the semi-final. Maz went out and smashed it apart with two tens, I think he got,' he laughs. 'I'm pleased to say it was one of those typical South Piha days where it's six foot, southwest onshore. Maz got a massive wave into the cove. Somehow, I came second.'

He says he enjoyed the challenge of contests, even though it did not come naturally to him.

'You really have to overcome some of your own anxieties to be able to get out in the water and keep a cool head, and get a few waves.'

The contest experience equipped Stu with enough knowledge to be able to assist Leia.

'Leia is a really good competitor. Her gymnastics training really set her up psychologically to deal with very intense moments. And I don't know how many times in the last few minutes of a heat she comes through with a bomb. You can't do that unless you've got a cool head and believe in what you're doing.'

Stu jokes that she's like her mother when it comes to surfing. Caro has made the finals at two nationals.

'In the Over-30s — I need to make that

The Millar family enjoys the afternoon in their backyard.

clear,' she laughs. 'When it comes to Piha, I just had to compete. Really, I was encouraging my kids to compete. I had to show them that you've got to do this kind of thing, even if you are terrified. Just give it a go. Yes, it's really hard and it's scary, but give it your best. It's all about experience.'

Caro says her dream for Leia and Portia is to help them realise their dreams. Stu has a different take on it when it comes to surfing.

'The dream for our kids, in terms of surfing, is about making sure they can surf good enough so that we can keep surfing,' he smiles. 'It's a little bit of a selfish dream, but we do something every weekend. If it's not surfing, then it's got to be snowboarding. Or maybe skateboarding or fishing. That's what

we love doing and we're set up well to do it.'

Before we paddle out, I ask Leia what's the most important thing in her life.

'To have fun and achieve things that I want to achieve, like my goals,' she says. 'I have goals, but I don't write them down — I just keep them in my head.'

I ask her if she has a goal to beat her friend and greatest rival, Chloe Groube, in the next contest.

'Yes, that's my goal every time,' she laughs. 'Just joking, just joking. Well, my goal is to win, so I guess that includes beating Chloe.'

THE LIFE OF ZEN

ZEN WALLIS — PIHA,

WEST AUCKLAND

I can tell it's Zen way down the beach. Not because of the cap he's wearing or the backlit golden locks flowing out from it. But because of the swarm of young surfers buzzing around him like he's found some magic bean.

One of the young grommets, Olly, sidles up to me and completely unprompted reveals that his mother can put her neck out just by sneezing. He imparts the fact and scurries off to join Zen's after-school group without even raising an eyebrow.

'What Zen has done with Olly through surfing has been amazing,' Olly's embarrassed mum tells me, shaking her head and laughing at her son's revelation. 'Zen has built his resilience. He used to get a hard time at school, but the resilience he has learnt in surfing has flowed across every other part of his life — his work in school, everything.'

Zen has taken it upon himself to be a positive part of the Piha community. He's found his calling as a surf instructor, coach and mentor.

—

The Wallis family is as synonymous with Piha as the fine black sand that creates its beaches. They wear their heart on their sleeves when it comes to the community. Occasionally, that has spilled over into heated debates and even polarised various factions, but there is no stripping away the positive influence they have had. And Zen embodies that.

Zen is a born-and-bred Piha local. He has spent his whole life here.

PREVIOUS SPREAD
Travel and surf
adventures have filled
Zen's days.

OPPOSITE
Surfing didn't come
easy to Zen — he says
perseverance paid off.

Wetsuits on constant
rotation.

ABOVE
Surf art in Zen's home
on Garden Road.

A shrine to music and
Zen's surf titles.

'Even my great-grandparents had a house just down over there on the beachfront,' he says, pointing towards the beach. 'I've got solid roots here. My grandfather had lots of brothers and at school you didn't mess with the Wallises. If you made a mistake and tried to bully them or others, then lunchtime would come around and you'd have five or six of them coming at you. There are some radical stories, but they didn't hesitate to stand up to bullies or for what was right.'

Zen's father Phil would come out and spend holidays at Piha when he was young.

'He learnt to surf hanging out with the Byers and surf crew from out here. My dad was younger than me when he bought his house. He put the time in, worked hard and managed to secure an awesome place. For years, he had a halfpipe in the garage; even before my time, the local kids would jump off the school bus to come and skate. It was an epic move on his part. We're super-grateful for what he's created here.'

Zen is 29 and has travelled all over the world, but loves Piha more than anywhere. He admits it does have its 'funny little dynamics' and 'a melting pot of people'.

I meet him on the balcony of a rustic wooden bush home, set on the side of a steep hill, pegged in place by a row of nīkau and surrounded by other native bush. The view of the beach is framed by the descending flanks of the valley and we can see waves rolling in between them.

He tells me this is his god-daughter's mum's place.

'I moved in with them for what we all thought would be a little while — that was six years ago,' he laughs.

Zen had coached Ann's children, Lloyd and Lucy, in surfing since they were very young.

Ann works in a leadership role for Air New Zealand and does shift work. She was battling to get the kids to school, trainings or music lessons at the time and asked Zen to move in and help out.

'That was an easy thing for me to fill in. I'd just help them deal with jobs that she couldn't do,' Zen recalls. 'Ann is an incredible human — nothing's impossible for her. She'll find a way. Her job in Air New Zealand is basically a problem-solver. When shit hits the fan, she fixes it. She has a heart of gold. An amazing person.'

A while after Zen moved in, Lucy had her baptism and asked Zen to be her godfather.

'I was stoked. I'm there for these guys through thick and thin anyway. They're very much family to me.'

Lucy and Lloyd are now in their early twenties. Zen occupies a mezzanine floor above the garage. His brother Tane is staying when I visit.

'I love that we're right here, pretty much on the beach, but tucked away, back out of sight on the hill,' Zen says. 'There are not many places in Piha that you get a sunset 365 days of the year.'

ABOVE
(Clockwise from left)
Training mode with Piha Surf School.

Olly and some groms learning the ropes.

Surfing into a cave at a secret spot.

It seems to be mostly about fun in the waves.

OPPOSITE
Local groms Milo and Zeke take a day off school to train with Zen.

He says Piha sunsets were always different and always beautiful. And Piha is renowned for its black iron sands — scorching through summer and mesmerising the rest of the time.

'I remember as a kid, we were having a gathering on the beach with bongo drums and all sorts,' he says. 'I remember swishing my hand through the sand and seeing little speckles of light coming out. It looked like light had been trapped in there and I'd just released it.'

Zen grew up fascinated by magnets and liked being able to pick up sand and play with it, to see the way the magnetic fields worked. But he also liked how that sand formed banks that would create surfable waves.

'The sand creates these surf banks that are often phenomenal. For a beach break, we get really long, peeling waves. All the swell that we get in here pushes these currents and helps to create long banks. We get waves that peel off The Camel, the Piha Bar, and then the big rock formations create their own waves and sheltered zones.'

Zen runs his own business, Piha Surf School, and often teaches beginners to surf. He says it doesn't matter if the surf is massive because Piha has these perfect little zones where it is completely safe.

'There's the big perception that Piha's surf is very dangerous, and that gets compounded by shows like *Piha Rescue*,' he tells me. 'Actually, at South Piha, to get sucked out in a rip, you usually have to go the whole length of

the beach and then around the corner and out to get into real trouble. Yes, we definitely get a lot of swell, so you feel the power of the ocean and that's what intimidates people.

'You definitely need to respect it, but I have no trouble teaching people of all ages how to utilise the beach and surf safely and really enjoy it.'

He says the ocean has life lessons for most people, and the first is learning to relinquish control when you experience a wipeout and to go with the flow for the two or three seconds that it takes.

'If you panic, that two or three seconds can seem like an eternity in your head. What you're physically capable of is much more than what that wave is going to dish out to you. It teaches you about your mental state — being able to deal with your emotions, learning to control them, learning about your breathing. It's a whole discovery journey that I've helped so many people take.'

And it has been transformative for his clients. Zen has watched people change their lives, change their jobs, move house — completely shift direction because of their experiences in the surf.

'They've gone from having a very depressive life where they're not enjoying it, not liking their job, wondering what life's about and what they're even doing, to loving life. They find this whole new world. They find themselves as a person and learn about how their emotions work.'

ABOVE
Zen, 22, and Tane, 19, at a surf contest in 2014, when Tane would rule the waves.

OPPOSITE
Zen and his younger brother, Tane check the surf.

—

Zen grew up in one of the most competitive age groups that surfing in New Zealand has ever seen.

'My brother, Tane, was the star — he was the superstar and I was in that second rank, a semi-finals kind of guy,' Zen recalls. 'I remember going through stages where I would lose the first heat at every contest, and for long periods. For me, it was about learning how to lose, how to get through and not give up.'

Tane was twice Under-14 National Surfing Champion and the 2012 Under-18 National Surfing Champion.

Zen's path through life has also weaved through some incredible achievements, including representing New Zealand in surfing nine times. He is the 2019 Oceania Champion; he was the coach of that same Oceania team when New Zealand won. He has multiple national titles, a number of open-contest wins, and he won the Volcom Qualifying Series (VQS) in 2011.

'No one would've picked me to have won that,' he smiles. 'Suddenly, I'm going off to California to compete in the VQS World Finals.'

That was when everything first started clicking for Zen. He went from being a B-grade surfer to winning everything, his hard work and solid foundation paying off.

'I found my self-belief through persistence.

It was like I had finally reached this level.'

Zen was also helped by his open mind and ability to 'cherry-pick' the qualities he admired in those around him.

'I knew I was a good human through and through, whether someone was watching or not,' he adds. 'I grew up believing in karma and had that reinforced so many times — when you do good things, good things happen. I'd seen so much evidence of it growing up. That made an impact.'

He says karma is a Hindu and Krishna-style belief system, and even though he never went to church every Sunday, he learnt bits from Christianity, and from his Hindu, Muslim, Krishna and spiritual friends around the planet.

'Travelling through the world, you meet all sorts of people, and I had a mum who was just spiritual in a whole different way. Some people call it God, other people call it Krishna, or Allah, and people like my mum would call it "the universe". They've all got values that can help you to become a better human.'

He says no one religion or spirituality outlook completely fitted with him enough for him to want to subscribe this way or that. He's always looking to learn and grow.

'That's something you have to learn for yourself as a human — how much are you just blindly following and how much are you thinking for yourself?' he asks. 'Take the good from everything you can and just be aware of what the negative is. I guess that's having

The coastline that has shaped Zen and his brother Tane.

your own moral compass. It applies to many things in life.'

Zen's goal has always been to enjoy life and make the most of any opportunities. That ethos was handed to him by his father, who took him on adventures around the world. Each journey, they'd meet his friends from all his travels.

'There's one story of him talking about when he was in Indo and all these little kids, they all just started calling him "For Love",' he beams. 'In these interactions that he'd have with all these little kids, as they were learning about tourists and surfing, he'd always tell them, "We do this for love." It's a little insight into the kind of human Dad is.'

Zen says he was 15 and Tane was 12 when

they did their first trip by themselves to Hawai'i.

'Dad's friends in Hawai'i picked us up and took us in. They showed us around the South Shore, and then we stayed with other friends up on the North Shore for the second part of our trip. Through seeing this we started creating our own connections. Now I've got friends all over the planet and from all walks of life.'

There are a few mottos that Zen lives by, and one of them has been in the family for generations.

'My great-grandfather used to say, "Don't waste time and energy on things you can't change." I know a lot of people who live in awesome places and have great lives and

everything, and yet they're fully depressed or unhappy with their lives. If you're looking at it, you might ask, "Okay, what is this issue? Can I change it?" Yeah? Then change it. If the answer is no, then it's just a part of this world and accept it. I know usually things aren't as simple as that, but it's a good foundation to build upon.'

Through his travels, Zen has also learnt that a lot of your trajectory depends on your attitude.

'Like on a plane. Whether you're pointing up or pointing down — your attitude. Your altitude is how high you are. You can be as high as anything and have a shit attitude, or be rock bottom with a good attitude and be completely happy. We got to see this travelling

to various countries where people don't have all the same things that we take for granted. They might live in a mud hut, but they're perfectly happy.'

After breaking up with his fiancée a few years ago, changing a lot of his plans and direction, Zen experienced a small bout of depression. He was a bit lost.

'I spent a couple of months with my best mate Storm in Indo,' he recalls. 'He would so often point out that it was someone's attitude that needed fixing, not the situation that was making a problem or getting them rattled. He'd usually do it through banter and laughter, and often about reasonably trivial things during our adventures. It was just this little idea, but a couple of months later

ABOVE
(Clockwise from left)
Zen takes his friend Iris
to a secret spot.

Zen is one of the great
surfers of New Zealand

Milo, Zeke, Zen and Iris
rock hopping to the
cove.

OPPOSITE
Zen waxes up before a
surf during a trip south.

it really sunk in for me and I used it to turn myself around. It took realising that I was a bit down first, and then I decided to change my attitude. A big thing for me was to focus on myself and keep doing things that would make me a better person. The next year was the best year of my life. The results showed through, too. That following year was the first time I'd ever been number one in the New Zealand surfing rankings for Open Shortboard and Longboard simultaneously.'

He understands that journey hasn't been so easy for other people.

'I love to help people and do what I can, but it does come down to each individual's choice around what they put their focus and attention on. All the help in the world won't do much if we don't choose to help ourselves.'

—

The next day, Zen takes his friend Iris, a German cliff-diving athlete, for a surf at a secret spot down the coast. He picks up two young surfers, Milo and Zeke, on the way in. He seems so happy to be on a surf adventure, sharing his backyard with someone new.

'Piha is just such a beautiful place. I will be out in the surf and look up at these hills and I still go, "Wow." Even though I've seen them my whole life.'

RIDING WAVES

MIKE AND LINLEY COURT —

WHALE BAY, RAGLAN

For many people, it is their passion for the sea that brings balance to their careers. For Mike and Linley Court, surfing has prescribed their extraordinary journey through life.

'One day, we decided to drive down to The Point to have a look,' Mike tells me, recalling the day surfing changed forever in Raglan. He was with his mate Campbell Ross and another friend, Grant Griffiths.

'Campbell, being a goofy footer and on his forehand, was the first guy to paddle out. He wasn't overly worried about the board getting smashed or anything — the rocks were pretty rugged-looking. Campbell got a couple of waves and it was all on from there — everybody was out there.'

It was the summer of 1961–62 and, to their knowledge, that was first time anyone had surfed The Point, Manu Bay. Up until then, surfing had only taken place at the beach —

The Point was just how they could tell if sets were coming.

'We never looked back from there. We still surfed the beach a bit on the very small days, but The Point was the place from that moment on.'

Mike, now 80, chuckles as he thinks back to those days and the trajectory it sent him on. His wife Linley smiles at the fond memories as she shuffles through some photo albums.

Their Whale Bay home stands above the breaking waves. Billie, their beloved nine-year-old dog, sits nearby. Outside the window, almost within touching distance, a new swell teases surfers.

—

Mike was born in Thames and spent his early years in Ngārimu Bay on the Thames Coast. His family ran a drapery shop in Thames. When Mike was 12, his father took off and left him, his mother and his two sisters behind. They moved into Thames, and it was there that Mike became very proficient at swimming, winning most of the Thames competitions at the time.

'My mother decided that we should move to Hamilton, where a well-respected New Zealand swimming coach, Bob Frankham, had a swim school,' he recalls. 'He invited me into the school and I swam for many years there in the mid-1950s, mainly freestyle. I held every freestyle record for a Waikato swimmer from thirty-three and a third yards to 1650 yards.'

Mike first became curious about surfing when he discovered a copy of *Popular Mechanics* featuring a drawing of a surfboard. He later met Peter Miller, a clubby from Mount Maunganui who was building these boards in a shed.

'I was down the road working for an insurance company and I got chatting with him, and said, "Oh, I'd really like one of those." He made me one and I first started surfing on it in 1959.'

Something about surfing grabbed Mike. The national swimming champs were to be held in Tauranga in 1959, but Mike spent his whole day in the ocean, surfing. Everyone expected him to become national champion, but he came third, mainly due to him being surfed out.

'That was bit of a let-down for my coach,' he remembers. 'That was the start of my transition. I got very intense with it, to the degree that I would come out to Raglan after work and sleep the night at The Point, with no one else around apart from my mother. She used to come out and get the board off the rocks for me. We'd both sleep in the car. I'd have another surf in the morning and then go back to work.'

That was before leg ropes were invented. The rocks created a new market: ding repairs.

'On a Friday night, the dinged boards would start to come in, and by Saturday, Sunday, Monday, they were just lined up at our house in Nixon Street in Hamilton,' he laughs. 'I'd rapidly repair the boards and send them out back to the owner. So I built up quite a clientele until the IRD got me.'

The Inland Revenue Department gave Mike 'a bit of a work-over' for his backyard board-repair business.

'I think somebody might have nobbled me. I did very well out of it. I probably bought my first house out of repairing boards.'

It was the catalyst for something bigger. Mike got to know the board shapers and became an agent for them in Hamilton and the general Waikato area. From that, he built up a retail business called Surf 'n' Gear. They first opened the shop in Hamilton East in 1967.

—

Mike had been working at an insurance company in the early 1960s when the company offered him a transfer to Melbourne in 1961.

After a stint there he was transferred back to Hamilton for a further five or so years. That is when he met his future wife, Linley. Mike soon realised that the insurance work wasn't fitting with him at all. He decided to leave and ended up in Coolangatta. Linley soon joined Mike on the Gold Coast. And not long after, Bob and Mary Davie made contact and invited them back to set up a surfboard factory on Barrys Point Road in Auckland. Mike's mother was still running Surf 'n' Gear in Hamilton.

They went in 50/50 from the start, the new factory and shop taking the Bob Davie Surfboards name in the spring of 1969. They had a retail shop at the front, which Linley ran. Rodney Davidson was another surfboard shaper on Barrys Point Road, and he and Mike

decided they would apply for a Saturday-morning trading licence.

'We went before the courts and had all the people groaning and moaning,' Mike smiles. 'There were about ten or twelve applications, and we were the only one to get a Saturday-morning trading licence — probably the first one in New Zealand.'

Linley said they sold the usual surf shop items: boards, wax, roof racks, and Mike's mother's calico board covers. In collaboration with Alan Langton, who made dive wetsuits up the road, they started making Moana Nui wetsuits when wetsuit technology first emerged. Then Hang Ten arrived.

'That was a revelation,' Linley recalls. 'For the first time ever, there was clothing especially for young people. Up until then, when kids started growing up they wore adult clothes — old people's clothes, because that was all there was to buy. Then Mary Davie started making her Surfset clothing and that just went crazy.

'Mary was also the first to use Velcro on the fly of her boardshorts — she and Bob were incredibly successful people. That was the beginning of it all for us.'

By 1973, Bob and Mary were looking for a change.

'Bob had the tiger by the tail. The business was romping,' adds Mike. 'It was really going off and the Surfset clothing was selling, then all of a sudden, out of the blue, "Right, pull me out of here. I'm going to Whangamatā."'

ABOVE
The Courts' home is positioned in the prime location to take in the view.

OPPOSITE
Mike and Linley with Billie.

The entranceway with a memorial to their late Labrador Millie.

The Courts' home aglow on a spring evening.

Mike and Linley bought the Davies' share of the business, and that same year surfboard shaper Pete Coggan came back from the States. He decided to go into partnership with them and they changed the name to Blue Spirit Surfboards.

In 1972, Mike and Linley had a son, James, and decided they wanted to move back to Hamilton. Pete and his wife, Mary, wanted to travel, so the group decided to put the business on the market and found a buyer.

'It was a bit of a stupid move, really,' Linley reflects.

When Mike and Linley got back to Hamilton, they weren't really sure what to do. At 35, Mike even considered becoming a builder's apprentice, because they had signed a restraint of trade when they sold the business. The only thing he really knew, or wanted to do, was to make boards. So they opened another shop at Mahana Road making surfboards, repairing boats, making fibreglass mouldings for campervan tops and Edwards skateboards.

Shortly after, they moved Surf 'n' Gear into Alexandra Street, in the centre of Hamilton, a much better location.

'It was probably one of the most successful surf shops in New Zealand,' Mike says.

Mike worked out of Mahana Road and would visit Raglan regularly to surf and fish. Around this time, he met Gerry Gerrand, who was keen to produce a fibreglass runabout. Together, they made the first tooling moulds for the Buccaneer — a very strong brand that is still running today.

'In return for my work and thinking, I pulled the first two boats out and set one up for myself and one up for my brother-in-law,' Mike recalls. 'He was living in Fiji and bought a motor there. When he came back, we set his boat up and we came out here fishing one day. We went around the corner here to Jacksons and the motor broke down.'

Jacksons Reef is just south of Raglan. With

the motor refusing to budge and a storm looming, they were helpless. By nightfall, things were worse.

'No one comes back from this coast,' Linley explains. 'The storm was raging and I kept thinking, *Well, where are they? There's nowhere to go.*'

'No one knew they'd gone, apart from Vivie, Mike's sister, and me,' Linley recalls. 'We lived next door to each other, and she rang me about ten at night and said, "Are those boys home?" I said, "No, they are at the pub and, boy, they are going to get it when they get home." And she said, "Oh, okay." We both went back to bed, and then about five minutes later she rang. And she said, "I think I might ring the police."'

She called back shortly after: the police had found the car and trailer. Because the storm was raging, they couldn't initiate a search.

'In those days, there was no TV in the middle of the night, but the All Blacks were playing, so we sat and watched the game,' remembers Linley. 'We waited for the morning, and then they put all the search parties out.'

'We drifted all night in a horrendous storm,' Mike recalls. 'We were really lucky, because we had been diving and had wetsuits on. We drifted all the way down to Kāwhia at Aotea Harbour in a big horseshoe direction. Around four or five o'clock in the morning, we ended up about half a mile off Gannet Rock, nineteen kilometres off the mainland. With

ABOVE
Mike Court holds a Morning Star surfboard that he built at his Mahana Road factory in Hamilton.

OPPOSITE
(Clockwise from left)
The axe-shaped Gannet Rock that the trio became marooned upon.

The front-page survival story — *New Zealand Herald*, 9 November 1981.

Photo from the actual rescue in 1981.

me being a reasonable swimmer, they tied a trawling line to me and I swam into the rock and tried to pull the boat in, but I couldn't — the storm was too bad. The boat went down on the reef. We ended up marooned on the rock. Before we knew it, we had helicopters and Orions flying around, but it was such shitty weather they couldn't see anything.'

A large trawler that had been sheltering from the storm down at Taharoa was steaming on its way home when the deckhand, who had just got a new camera with a telephoto lens, was trying it out on the rock.

They were brought aboard and transferred to another trawler to return to Raglan.

'That really affected me,' Mike recalls, gazing out to sea. 'I came back and I said

to them, "I'm out of this fibreglass game." We sold the business building to Gerry and concentrated on the retail business in town.'

After his near-death experience, Mike helped Linley at the shop.

'That's really when it started to flourish, because I had been trying to juggle family and the shop up until then,' Linley recalls. 'With Mike involved, I could just focus on the buying and presentation of the shop, while Mike did all the foot work — it worked really well.'

The owner of the menswear shop next door had just visited Australia and noted that the boardshort market was 'going crazy' there. He encouraged Mike and Linley to look into it.

'Rena and Gordon Merchant were just making the clothing in a house then,' Mike says of the Billabong founders. 'We went over there, met up and bought some stock from them.'

Linley remembers the boardshorts barely hit the shelves before they were swept up by customers. It was 1984 and rainbow-coloured Billabong boardshorts were in. They knew there was something about the Billabong brand, so they decided to approach Gordon for the licence.

Mike realised he'd need some staff to pull that off, and teamed up with John Snelling, who had worked for a company that had just gone broke and was at a loose end.

'We sat there in Gordon Merchant's office and tried to get him interested in the idea,' Mike recalls. 'He wasn't so sure about it. He wasn't keen. However, Alan Byrne had worked for me and knew me very well. He put in a good word for me. So Gordon said, "Okay, guys, you can have a go." And that was the start of the Billabong operation.'

With the brand under licence, they set about making the gear here in New Zealand in 1986. The three partners put in 'an awful lot of really, really hard work'. Trying to make product in New Zealand at that stage proved to be very difficult.

Every year, they would have to go to the Gold Coast to the Billabong headquarters for meetings with all the licensees. Mike remembers one year in the mid-1990s when things changed.

'Gordon sat up there and he said, "Well, guys, I'm shutting all the manufacturing plant down in Australia. We're going to China." He was probably one of the first guys to go into China.'

Mike said the profits were out of sight, but so too were the risks.

'We were dealing with the Chinese and had no quality control. This is the whole Billabong operation worldwide.'

Mike used to pull samples from the supply with every shipment.

'I can remember once we had a thousand men's shirts. I got my samples in the office and tried one on and a whole bloody sleeve fell off. It was all history — the whole order. And, of course, we'd already paid for it and paid GST for the whole lot. To recover the GST, you had to destroy all the garments. It was hard work, but that's just the cost of doing business offshore.'

'In the end, they set up really good quality control,' Linley adds.

From that point on, Billabong ran along very profitably, amassing about 25 staff under Mike, Linley and John Snelling. Their early success encouraged Billabong's 'international man' Dougall Walker to introduce them to Oakley CEO Mike Parnell, who was looking for a distributor for Oakley in New Zealand in 1988.

'We didn't know anything about Oakley . . . who the bloody hell was Oakley?' laughs Mike. 'Mike Parnell came out and met John and me at our little office above Kevey Panelbeaters on Barrys Point Road. Mike Parnell pulled out some of the product — there were ski goggles and things like that. I'm looking around with this, wondering what to say. Then Grant Kevey the panelbeater walked by — he was a keen skier. He asked, "Mike, what are those?" I told him they were Oakley ski goggles. "Mate," he said, "they are top of the line. Jesus, can I get some of those?" That's when John and I realised this might be interesting.'

They agreed to 'have a crack at it' and started negotiating. Linley took a particular interest in the new brand and soon became the 'Oakley lady'. She built a solid reputation focused on customer service, and the brand exploded in New Zealand.

'She had so much product going out the door. It was just amazing,' says Mike. 'I'd go to a rugby game and I'd look around and there'd be all these Frogskins looking back at me.'

—

Local surfer Daniel Kereopa surfs at Manu Bay where, almost 60 years earlier, Mike's friend Campbell Ross first ventured out.

We take a walk down the steps, through their garden to the front gate, which is flanked by trees. It opens up onto the Whale Bay foreshore like a secret door to another world. Waves roll by with surfers carving from top to bottom, hooting, cheering and occasionally getting clipped by the lip. A stream of surfers run around the track to Indicators, and sightseers mill about on the rocks.

'We're the lucky generation all the way through,' Linley says. 'Even to this Covid thing — most of us are retired, we don't have to worry about jobs or anything. We have missed out on wars — we have missed out on everything. We've had this dream life. We really have had a dream run.'

Mike leans in and adds to that: 'And we've

had massive increases in property value over the years.'

Linley notes that it has been especially tough in a place like Raglan, which was always an affordable place for average Kiwis to come and live or retire.

The dream run for Mike and Linley began to unravel when Billabong was publicly listed on the Australian Securities Exchange on 11 August 2000. Within the year, Oakley also went public. That left Mike and Linley with some decisions to make.

'We were approached by Billabong to either continue our licence and work under this public umbrella, or they would buy us out,' recalls Mike.

They decided to move sideways.

OPPOSITE
The terraced garden,
which eventually
claimed Mike's back.

ABOVE
Mike, Linley and Billie
enjoy their rocky
backyard.

Photo albums capture
the extraordinary life of
the Court duo.

'I was sixty going on sixty-one, and John was pretty keen to sell, too,' Mike says. 'As part of the agreement, we were paid out a certain fund and given an application for shareholding in the new Billabong operation. It was a good outcome for us.'

The dust hadn't even settled from that upheaval when Linley came into the upstairs office with an email from Oakley.

'It just read: "Sorry guys, it's all over — we're taking over the New Zealand operation."' Mike shakes his head. 'Just one sentence and we are all sitting there looking at it thinking, *You've got to be kidding.*'

It was in stark contrast to the way Billabong had handled the situation.

'Financially, it was okay, but it certainly wasn't as generous as the Billabong operation,' Mike recalls. 'So within one year, our whole thing had gone, but we were happy with that. We had other projects.'

'We had worked hard. We were well and truly ready,' Linley adds.

That's when they decided to relocate their beloved fibro bach, which they had bought in 1986 for about $70,000, up the road so they could build their new home at Whale Bay.

They now divide their time between their three homes in the triangle of Auckland, Whangamatā and Raglan.

'We spend a lot of time in Auckland. We have boats and things,' Mike explains. 'But Raglan tends to be our anchor.'

The Whale Bay home was an incredible build that made the most of the north-facing aspect and steep site. But when they finished it, something still wasn't right.

'We weren't happy with it,' Linley tells me. 'It just made me angry. We'd have guests over and we'd be sitting in there looking at the wall, when you've got one of the best views in New Zealand sitting right here.'

The view had been shut off from the main lounge and almost sealed off by a straight line of windows. To remedy it, they expanded out

towards the view and created a second space
that appreciates the lines of swell wrapping
along Whale Bay and captures the west coast's
spectacular light.

The garden is terraced down to the bay
with wooden steps, decks and mini-spaces all
planted out thoughtfully. Mike built it all.

'This is why I'm struggling in the mornings
with my back,' he tells me. 'It was coming up
to Christmas, so I camped out here and just
continued to work on it. Then I woke up one
morning and I couldn't move. I ended up in
the hospital with a major operation on my
back.'

I ask Linley what it's like when she has her
son James and daughter Ainsley to visit. She
shakes her head.

'Well, once again, it's not built for a family.
But when ten of us are here, we can do it,
but it's not ideal. That's not entirely the
architect's fault. We built this when we didn't
have any grandchildren. Now we've got all
these cute girls — life changes.'

—

As the sun is dropping in the sky, we take up
a spot on the deck and pour a drink. Mike tells
me that he wishes he was a bit younger.

'I tell you what, there are some things you
can't beat and one of them is old age.'

We watch a set roll through and can hear
the lip rumble and crack along the rocks.
Mike, who won a lot of surf contests in his day,
tells me he no longer surfs. He remembers
the point in his life where he stopped surfing
altogether.

'It was horrible,' he tells me, shaking his
head. 'It was one day out here. I'd gone out for
a surf and there was only three of us in the
water. There was my next-door neighbour's
daughter, Yjosina, and one other guy. I'd had a
couple of waves and I was feeling a bit sore in
my back. I was just paddling back out and this

ABOVE
Last light through
Whale Bay.

OPPOSITE
Mike watches a set
peel through Indicators
from his crow's-nest
bedroom.

Minimalist design at the
rear of the house.

Tākapu translates to
gannet, the name of
the rock that saved
Mike's life.

monster set came through and just totalled me — about eight waves. You have to roll over to get under them, and at about the third wave I just lost it. My back gave out and I ended up on the rocks down here. Yjosina saw I was in trouble; she came alongside me and managed to get me on the rocks down here. Then Linley came running down and said, "It's about time you gave it up." So I did. It's really frustrating, but I think you've got to grow old gracefully and I wasn't growing old gracefully by doing that.'

'It is very hard for him to sit here and watch it,' Linley adds. 'It was like torture for him there for a while.'

'I'm okay now, but there are still days when the surf is perfect and I can't even watch,' he says. 'I will just go into my workshop.'

Linley confides in me that she has one regret.

'I'm kicking myself now that I didn't surf. I see these girls now and I just get this feeling I missed something special.

'We've been a good partnership,' Linley adds. 'We've worked together really well. We've had an extraordinarily exciting life, but not without taking risks. We've always consulted with each other a lot. Whenever we made a move, we were both on the same page.

'Ignorance is bliss, too. If someone told me to start doing what we did, you'd say, "No way." You do what you have to do, because there's no alternative.'

WELCOME TO GROUBELAND

If a boardriding-obsessed teenager had the opportunity to design their dream house, then Matt and Amber's home in Pāuanui would come very close. We're talking four skateboard ramps, one at 13 sheets of plywood wide, all undercover, a skate park-inspired concrete driveway, a pool that can be drained for skating, a fully equipped gym and a gymnast's trampoline. This is all set on the flank of a hill overlooking the township and surf peaks of Pāuanui. Welcome to Groubeland.

Matt Groube is now 48, but he was six months old when his parents sold their Matamata dairy farm and moved to the beach.

'My mum found this place in the seventies and she brought my dad here and said, "We're going to buy this land."' Matt laughs as we lounge around in the afternoon sun in his cabana. 'He told her she was a lunatic because

there was nothing here. What was ever going to come of it?'

Along with the 185 acres of land, they bought the first original shop that was in Pāuanui. They ran a takeaway alongside it and hired mini motorbikes and miniature ponies to visitors. Matt grew up hanging around the shop.

They eventually sold the shop, and Matt's dad, Arthur, went to work in forestry in the steep hills around the town. Arthur could never sit still and started to do the odd tree job around town as well.

'He had a full-on tree business before you knew it,' Matt recalls. 'I left school when I was fifteen and started working for him. I've done that ever since.'

Matt started skating when he was 11 and surfing when he was 12 — school took a back seat after that. He was 18 when he discovered snowboarding, among one of the first wave of snowboarders in New Zealand, in 1994. He quickly became one of New Zealand's leaders in the emerging snowboard movement, living in Ōhakune each winter, right through until he was 30.

'I always kept an eye on the weather map and came home when the surf was good,' Matt remembers. 'I travelled backwards and forwards between the two, because I didn't like to miss out on surfing. Then I'd work for my dad when I came back.'

Matt always had an individual style on the mountain and carved himself an

PREVIOUS SPREAD
The Groube family have married their obsession with boardriding to the laidback beach lifestyle of Pāuanui.

OPPOSITE
Matt has a few finishing touches to go on his new board room.

ABOVE
(Clockwise from left) Matt and Chloe debrief after a final at the Whangamatā Grom Comp.

Matt spots his landing while testing his new foamy at Raglan.

Van life for the Groube family and friend Maya Mateja.

Lola can't help but smile in the waves.

impressive chapter in the history books — particularly in transforming Tūroa ski field into a snowboard-friendly slope. His pinnacle achievement was being invited to the Quiksilver Cup surf, snow, skate event in Europe, alongside 20 of the world's best riders, including Omar Hassan, the Fletcher brothers and Shaun White.

'The surf was huge — ten to fifteen foot, and the snowboard side of it was a super park with big kickers and a super pipe. It was pretty gnarly. The standard was high.'

He ended up finishing ninth overall. After 10 years, Matt had had enough of snowboarding. It had lost its 'buzz' for him. He came home, worked full-time and took over the running of the tree business.

'Dad still works with me every day — he's eighty-two,' explains Matt. 'He'll still pick up the big saw and chainsaw all day. He's been chainsawing since he was fifteen — that's nearly seventy years. When we drop a big tree, I've got to be on the grapple, feeding the chipper, because I'm the only one who knows how to drive that machine. The other young fulla, he's got to stand on the chipper because it's quite physical getting the branches to bend to fit in there. So my dad limbs the trees up — he walks around and cuts every branch off. These trees are big — hundred-foot pines with huge branches. He goes hard all day.'

—

Around 2005, a young Amber Cordero finished her degree in the United States and went travelling with a girlfriend. They ended up in New Zealand using a house in Pāuanui as a base for their explorations around the country and in Australia. Towards the end of their trip, they were a bit low on cash. Matt offered them some work feeding trees into the chipper.

'I didn't know that Matt had a crush on me then,' Amber smiles. 'We exchanged numbers and I went back to the States. Then Matt came out to visit me. We did a big roadie from Northern California down to Mexico — it was super-fun. I didn't know at the time, but that was quite a big deal for Matt to come out for three weeks, to just hang with some chick in California.'

Matt invited Amber, then 24, back to New Zealand. She knew they had a spark and decided to give New Zealand a go. She spent a year and a half in Pāuanui and really loved it. Then she fell pregnant. Chloe was born in 2008. Lola came a few years later in 2011.

'Once you live in a place like this and you have kids, it changes the whole experience,' Amber tells me. 'All of a sudden, you meet other parents, go for walks on the beach and take the kids to swim in the estuary. It's just amazing. It is such a cool spot to raise kids.'

Until Covid, she had taken the girls each year to the States to see her family. Matt hadn't been on one trip, until about six years ago when he decided to meet them in Hawai'i on their way back. That became an annual family tradition.

Amber said those trips ignited Chloe's and Lola's surfing passion.

'Three weeks in Hawai'i riding Waikiki, perfect little A-frames, sunny, warm — it's so good for their confidence,' Matt says. 'Surfing three times a day, out of the hotel and straight into the surf. You could see the improvement every time we came back from that trip.'

Chloe is already one of New Zealand's top

surfers in her age group. Lola's an equally
fierce competitor in hers. They had just
started to travel to Australia to compete there
when Covid derailed their plans.

—

Matt and Amber lived in the original cottage
— the same house Matt moved into as a baby,
and the very first house in Pāuanui — until
they decided to start from scratch in 2006.

'We were dating and I was staying in Matt's
house,' Amber says. 'The rooms were so cold
and draughty, with only a little fireplace,
which heated the lounge. You'd go to the
bathroom and there were actual plants
growing through the walls.'

'When we pulled it down, we realised it
was insulated with rat's nests,' Matt laughs.
'All the walls were stacked full of grass and
hay and whatever else they'd dragged in. All
the walls, the roof, everything — just all rats.
They'd eaten through all the wires. It was
lucky it never burnt down.'

He said there had always been rat
problems, but it was never an infestation.

'You have to remember, this house has
been here since dot,' he says. 'And I was going
snowboarding for six months of the year. I
would just leave it locked up and go down
to the snow and then come back to it. It was
like a bach. We found all sorts; rats grab
everything — marbles, toys, plastic soldiers,
pens. It was bizarre. It was an archive. I

found stuff that I'd lost when I was a kid and I remembered losing, like little toy soldiers and marble sets and knuckle bones. They'd dragged them in there.'

He says it had been a bit emotional knocking it down. They had little option — the whole house had sunk around the fireplace and was bending with gaps in the floorboards. It was bitterly cold.

Matt says an old Māori guy had built it and lived there in the 1940s.

'He used to have a whole lot of cows here; milk them in the morning and trolley the cream down to a little boat that he had, put it on the boat and row it across to Tairua. He'd drop it off and get paid. That's how he survived.'

The new house is a modest, open-plan beach house design, positioned to take in the Coromandel sun and sheltered from the south.

'After living in that old house, having this is luxury,' Matt smiles.

Each time Amber and the girls went to the States, Matt would build a new feature. The first was a mini-ramp for skating, complete with a volcano on the wall.

'When they came back, I said, "Welcome to skateboarding, girls. You're gonna learn to skate."'

The next trip, he built the pizza-oven area. Then the pool. Then he joined two big sheds together and built another big ramp inside that one. Then he laid the driveway with specialist concrete designed for skating with

obstacles and kickers in each corner.

'It was a staged project,' he tells me.

The most recent addition is the covered deck area where we're sitting, and alongside that he's added a built-in trampoline.

'I've still got to finish the board shed. Then we'll move on to the pump track, which will start just by Chloe's bedroom and loop in front of the house to the front piece of grass. You'll be able to skate completely around.'

Groubeland has already attracted skaters from throughout New Zealand.

'In the beginning, it was madness, but awesome,' Matt recalls. 'The kids were into it and I was into it. I was skating heaps and I wanted people to skate with. Guys my age were still skating and they'd bring their kids. So every weekend without fail there would be thirty to forty people here. Full-on, non-stop, all day long. From eight o'clock in the morning until twelve o'clock at night sometimes. I used to light the pool up, so the pool would be all go. It was crazy.

'People would be walking through my house and we didn't even know them. Some kids would just turn up — it was a circus.

'Then it started to get a bit too much. We'd have five carloads of people turning up — mates of mates, but we didn't know them at all. They'd all pile out and there'd be beer bottles left behind. These days, if we're going to skate, we're surf-training skating.'

Life changes and with the girls doing so well in surf contests, that became a focus for the Groube family.

'A few years ago, we decided to buy a campervan and now we're hardly ever home,' Amber tells me. 'We have become so committed to travelling to where the waves are and taking the kids surfing.'

They surf all over the country and enjoy their time in the water together.

'There are not many sports that you can go out in the water and your kids are with you,' Matt says. 'Mum's on a wave, and then Dad's

on a wave — all four of us surfing.'

'Or Dad snaking everyone and taking all the waves,' Amber laughs. 'Sometimes we're all out there and I'm just looking around and thinking, *Wow. How amazing is that? How blessed are we? Does life get any better than this?* It's pretty magical.'

Pāuanui does not have the best reputation for wave quality, and that suits Matt and his family.

'When Whangamatā Bar and other waves are pumping, then usually Pāuanui is, too,' he says. 'It's not incredibly consistent, but when it's good, it's as fun as you'd ever want.'

He says the peaky north swells and straight east swells are the best, while southeast swells ran a bit fat along the beach.

'We've got some good spots up the coast. Point breaks, reef breaks, a couple of secret spots we reach on a ski. Then we've got world-class Whanga Bar right there, which we surf a lot. That's our go-to break. We try not to miss it. If that means the girls get pulled out of school a few days in a row, well, that's what happens.'

Every member of the family is a goofy footer, so they love surfing left-handers like Whangamatā Bar and Raglan. Manu Bay at Raglan is a favourite.

'People poke a bit of fun at Manu Bay, but I reckon, with where we're at with our kids and with the campervan, you can't get any better,' he says. 'You pull up there on a sunny day with a campervan and they're surfing,

skating, doing walks, doing jump rock, hanging with their friends, they come in and get food. It's as good as it gets anywhere in the world. Kids can paddle out with dry hair and surf a two-hundred-metre-long left-hander. It's an amazing spot.'

—

There is no question the Groubes live an enviable lifestyle, but they've shed some blood to get there.

'There are a lot of hard yards that have gone in behind where we're sitting at the moment,' Matt tells me. 'It hasn't been rainbows the whole time, that's for sure. I think we've been through four mortgagee sales on the properties over the years. We were land-rich, but never income-rich.'

The crash of 2008 and the ensuing global financial crisis nearly ended the Pāuanui dream. The bank panicked, closed on them and forced a mortgagee sale of their entire property portfolio.

'They just got taken from us,' Matt remembers. 'It was hectic. I had to buy this back — I had to actually go to the mortgagee sale and stand in line. We're good now, but it was a graft. They were some shit years, just horrible . . .'

Amber suggests jokingly that's why he lost his hair.

Matt says it was his girls, and being able to surf, that pulled him through the dark days.

'When you go through stuff like that,' begins Amber, 'it's so gnarly, but it makes you appreciate everything so much more.'

It changed Matt's outlook as well.

'When I go out in one-foot waves and I see a wave that's barrelling, I'm stoked,' he says. 'It doesn't have to be six foot and pumping. You don't have to be riding the best wave to have the time of your life. You go through stuff that puts it all into perspective. The struggle was worth it.'

—

Later, while the kids lap around the pool on their SmoothStar surf-trainer skateboards, Amber tells me about her business, the New Zealand Natural Pet Food Company, which she set up with her friend, Jac Taylor, four years ago.

Matt claims he helped name the dog and cat brands, Woof and Meow. Amber laughs.

'We're about to launch into the States,' she tells me. 'That'll be the eleventh country that we are in. We've grown it really slowly, but in a really sustainable way. It's all made right here in New Zealand.'

When they first developed the concept, they wanted to take the natural goodness of New Zealand and share it with the world. The concept has been a success. It also helped Amber leave her real estate job and join the Groube family adventures.

'There's a reason why we live here and that's to enjoy the lifestyle,' she says. 'So I had to make the decision to take a pay cut for a little bit, knowing that I'm going to be doing something that I love.'

Matt has also developed a brand, Neon Surf, producing quality foam surfboards for an entirely new and growing market segment in surf. He's worked with surfboard shaper Pete Anderson to produce what he believes is the best foam surfboard on the market.

'I've got a brand, but I don't know how far

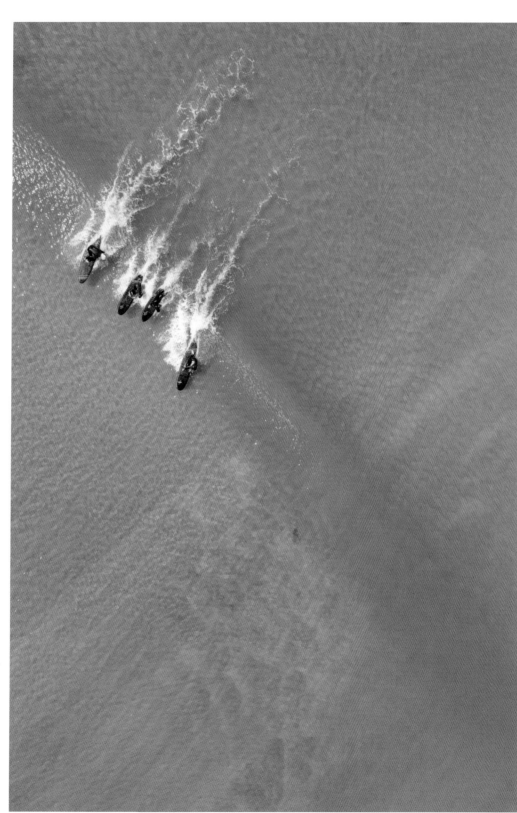

RIGHT
The Groube family
balances the pressure of
contests with the fun of
riding foam surfboards
at home.

OPPOSITE
The Groube family enjoy
time together at their
local break in Pāuanui.

Pauanui is one of the
hidden gems of the
Coromandel.

Pāuanui at dawn.

NEXT SPREAD
Amber and Matt check
the surf early one
morning.

we will go with it. I'm not money-orientated — I just want to have fun with it,' he says. 'I'm okay if it doesn't go well.'

Amber tells me that Matt just wants to share the fun.

'He's so passionate about wanting everyone to have a good time.'

Matt and Amber agree that their lifestyle is perfect right now. Covid really drove home for them how little they actually need to be happy.

'If you can get rid of your debt and you don't have money hanging over your head, driving you every day, then it's a nicer feeling,' Matt says. 'There are still the hassles of life that everyone goes through — whatever's going on in your life. But if you can get rid of that real hunk of debt hanging over your head, it's definitely a better lifestyle.'

Amber said it bought them the freedom to choose what they wanted to do: 'You're not chained to anything.'

Matt's attitude has proven contagious, especially among the younger surfers in town.

'The local boys idolise Matt — he's like Peter Pan out in the waves, hooting and hollering when he gets his little one-foot barrels,' smiles Amber.

Matt puts it down to his ambition just to have fun.

'If you have a good attitude towards them, you give them the time of day and you're having fun, then why wouldn't they?' he says. 'And it's all about them. It's all about the next lot of kids coming through.'

Matt and Amber pause for a minute and reflect on where they are.

'You know when you're so comfortable somewhere that you couldn't physically live anywhere else,' Matt says. 'I've travelled around the world. I've been a few places and look at what's happening in the world right now. Where would you be right now? We're in the spot.'

CHILDREN OF THE LAKE

Ōkere Falls, near Lake Rotoiti, is a breeding ground for river and lake kids. They are afforded a semi-rural, mostly adventure-seeking childhood that weaves something magical into their minds and ambitions. Some suggest they have the spirit of the lake within them.

As I wind my car towards the Ryan family home perched above Te Weta Bay, the road draws narrower and the bush closes in overhead like a corridor to another world.

The Ryans' house is wedged between the trees like it was always meant to be there. Through the front door and down the hallway, you're greeted by an open, expansive kitchen and lounge. Just beyond, a deck spills out onto a small lawn with an infinity edge to the bush and bay below.

Blackberry, or Blackers, the family's 13-year-old cat, squirms around upside down

PREVIOUS SPREAD
Lewis Ryan and his
partner Suné explore the
shoreline of Lake Rotoiti,
near the Ryan family
home.

OPPOSITE
The family home juts
out into the bush
overlooking a bay in
Lake Rotoiti.

ABOVE
The indoor–outdoor
flow of the Ryans' home
matches their lifestyle.
The spa pool gets plenty
of use.

in the grass. Cooper, their dog, takes higher ground on the outdoor sofa next to Brendan and Karen. Their son Lewis warms up in the spa after a lake swim with his partner Suné. And Ruby reminisces about their childhood adventures. Lewis and Ruby are both exceptional endurance athletes and compete throughout the world.

—

Karen and Brendan used to own a little yacht and had spent time exploring Lake Rotoiti. They enjoyed their time in the sheltered Te Weta Bay. They moved to the lakes when Lewis was one — more than 20 years ago.

'We looked at all the lakes, and then we just chose Rotoiti because there was so much to do here,' Karen smiles. 'We liked having the hot pools and the length of the lake with all the little bays appealed. And it is so close to the Kaituna River.'

Karen said the bay also had a really interesting Māori history.

'Directly opposite our house, on that far bank there, are food caves hidden in the bush,' she explains, waving her hand across the bay. 'You can actually climb through the caves. It was a pā site, and, in this bay, they planted a lot of kūmara. Māori canoes used to come through the Ōhau Channel to try and raid the kūmara grounds.'

Karen smiles as she remembers they had friends who rented the house many years ago.

'We used to keep our yacht here on the jetty, and then they moved out but we left the yacht here. We never knew the people who owned it. We kept coming out to use it. One day, we came out and they were here. They had been wondering whose yacht it was. It was quite cheeky . . . very Kiwi.'

The owners were from Wellington and were 'really nice' people. They were older with children living overseas, and they wanted to sell.

'So, we bought this tiny little Lockwood house,' Karen recalls. 'It had a big water tank, a little deck, and you couldn't even see the lake. There were no windows facing the lake. We've added on a couple of times and slowly made it our home.'

Over the past 20 years, Karen and Brendan have watched Ōkere Falls transition from 'a few oldies who had retired here to their baches' to be more permanent residential. With that, the road traffic has increased noticeably.

Ōkere Falls gets its reputation from the rafters and kayakers who make their living on the Kaituna River. The Kaituna empties Lake Rotoiti, just around the corner from Te Weta Bay.

'When summer kicks in, there's a big summer atmosphere out here,' says Karen. 'That kicks in for December and January. We're pretty pleased to see the back of that when February comes around.'

'The prices have definitely gone up,' says

ABOVE
Ruby, Ryan, Suné and friend Zack Mutton explore the lake by kayak.

OPPOSITE
Ruby tries the geothermally cooked beans.

Making the most of Lake Rotoiti's treasures.

Lewis leaps into the Kaituna River.

Brendan, who works in real estate and has his finger on the pulse.

'A lot of these lake-edge houses stay in families. They're in family trusts and they just get passed down. But non-lake-edge stuff in Ōkere Falls is kind of achievable for first-time buyers and rafting crew and people like that. It is not really expensive, so that's good. And that's why there's a good vibrancy in the community. It's really healthy — a good mix.

'That is changing rapidly,' he adds. 'Tauranga people are starting to buy holiday homes — it's much closer and easier for them now with the new highway.'

The Ryans' plan initially was to live here until Lewis went to school, at which point they'd move into town. That never happened.

'Once you're here, you never want to go back to living in town,' Karen smiles.

Sports might have proved difficult for the kids if it wasn't for the fact that both Karen's and Brendan's parents live in Lynmore. That happens to be right next to Whakarewarewa Forest, where all the mountain biking takes place.

'We were surrounded by other families who did kayaking, but we went mountain biking,' Lewis explains. 'We never had that burning need to try and be a white-water kayaker, but I have spent a lot of time kayaking on the lake over the years, for training and also for fun.'

Karen admits that living in Rotorua is about two things: the mountain biking and the lakes.

'It's about lakes and forests — the outdoors,' Brendan smiles. 'And it is close to the coast. Papamoa is thirty-five minutes away and we can be on the beach and we can go and get fish and chips.'

Brendan used to dabble in Xterra races, like backcountry triathlons with the adventure dial turned right up. His swim training took place in the lake right in front of his house.

'It was one kilometre return to a rock around the corner,' he explains. 'Or

1.5 kilometres if you swam to the power pole. The only danger was the swans. Sometimes if you were swimming on your own, you'd get attacked.'

To quell the attacks, one person would kayak alongside to keep the swans away while the other swam.

One day, Lewis was in training for an Xterra race and had to do his training swim alone.

'It was the only time I've done the swim without anyone kayaking beside me,' he recalls. 'I came for a breath. I breathe to the left, and I felt something hit my head from the right and then there was the noise of the wings and they're going for it. I was wearing a thick five-millimetre wetsuit around my body, and, even then, my back was pretty bruised up. They're seriously strong and it was just relentless.

'I was so dizzy, and I had drunk so much water. I didn't realise whether I was above or underneath the water with the panic of it all. I came up and these things were striking at me. I genuinely thought I was drowning.'

'That was really scary,' Karen adds. 'All of a sudden, I hear him call out, "Mum! Mum!"'

Karen ran to him and dragged him to the grass. He could hardly breathe.

'I actually stuck him in recovery position here on the lawn. I probably should have taken him to the hospital.'

'There aren't many downsides to living by the lake, apart from the swans,' Lewis grimaces.

Karen moved to the lakes from Wellington when she was about four. She lived at Lake Ōkareka and that's where she experienced her first swan attack.

'I've never forgotten it. I don't like them either.'

Karen works in town at a bike store, NZO Ride Central. She jokes that it is to feed their 'mountain bike habit'. I'm not sure she's joking.

ABOVE
The Ryan home is
always a busy place,
with two adult athletes
and two parents working
hard.

OPPOSITE
Sharing a meal together.

Making brunch.

Nine-year-old Cooper
— calm as you can get.

Life at Ōkere Falls is blissful. Lewis and
his sister Ruby roam with groups of friends,
swimming, kayaking and exploring the lakes
and rivers. Ruby's friend Rivey Mutton lives
near the Kaituna headwaters and they used to
kayak a lot together.

There are a range of cliff jumps into the
Kaituna near the Trout Pools, and every
Christmas Eve, Ruby and her friends would
swim down the Kaituna. The natural hot pools
around Lake Rotoiti are another favourite of
the Ryan family. Manupirua Hot Pools are a
15-minute boat ride from the jetty. A little
hot-water stream bubbles out of the bank
across the lake from their house.

Karen said that along with the swans
there were other downsides to living there,
including semi-regular power cuts, high
repair bills because of their distance to town,
and the general upkeep to the property.

'We're on water tank, so you are cleaning
your gutters a lot,' she says. 'And there is a
lot of gardening. But in the summer, you do a
bit of gardening and go down and have a swim
and then you wander back up. I just spend all
day in my togs.'

—

Lewis and Ruby grew up like rural kids. Lewis
remembers his thirteenth birthday for all the
wrong reasons.

'We went into this place that was like a
farm with log cabins — a real cool spot,' he

recalls. 'I took a bunch of mates there and we made a campfire, cooked dinner and roasted marshmallows. We had seen a video online where someone had put a Lynx can on the fire and it went up like a whoosh. It looked really cool. We thought we'd give that a whirl. Our Lynx explosion was so bad — this big heavy steel fireplace went boom and tipped completely over.'

Lewis's parents were so angry they made them pack up the whole adventure right there and went home.

Ruby said she had so many memories from growing up here, including a few near-death experiences.

'My *Dream Long Jump* idea was not a good one,' she recalls.

'Ruby had a Nintendo game called *Dream Long Jump*,' Lewis explains. 'The general concept was that you did this long jump, and if you went through these rings you got an extra boost to see how far you could go.'

They decided to bring it to real life one day.

'We had this really steep bank and there was this massive run-up, and it was straight out of *Dream Long Jump*,' Ruby laughs.

'Ruby and my friend Milo would run and jump as far as we could,' Lewis adds. 'Now, when we go down there, we look at it and we're just like, "Man, we used to land down here?" It was a terrible idea.'

It ended when Ruby nearly broke her neck and Milo hurt his knee so badly he ended up in a wheelchair for a time.

ABOVE
(Clockwise from top) Ruby is a world-class XC mountain-bike racer. Here she trains in Whakarewarewa Forest.

Training in the lakes of Rotorua has helped Lewis to become a formidable endurance athlete.

Ruby with her eighteenth-birthday bike . . . on its maiden ride.

NEXT SPREAD
Lake Rotoiti has been a playground for the Ryan family.

They built a tree hut and taught themselves, through trial and error, how to abseil. They loaded kayaks beyond capacity (which turned out to be eight of their mates), and once paddled all day for Mokoia Island in Lake Rotorua. They hung on for their lives on the biscuit behind the boat, learnt to waterski and wakeboard. They pioneered new jump rocks around the lake. They'd kick soccer balls off the lawn to their friends in the lake below. This was everyday entertainment for them.

'We used to do this for hours every day after school, and we all looked forward to it,' Ruby says.

Lewis, who barely knew how to sail, once decided to teach Ruby how to sail during a wild storm and freezing weather out on the lake. How they didn't get hypothermia remains a mystery.

'Mum and Dad have always let us do these things,' Lewis smiles.

—

After a lunch of waffles, we decide to kayak across the lake to heat some cans of beans in the geothermal river on the far side at Tūmoana Bay. Lewis and Ruby are joined by Suné and family friend Zack Mutton for the mission. Cooper hitches a ride, too.

I take the opportunity to ask Lewis about how he went from being a rising star in New Zealand cross-country mountain biking to chasing the Xterra pathway. Ruby is quick to offer her assessment.

'The real reason?' she asks, glancing across to Lewis. 'You weren't good enough.'

Lewis shakes his head and laughs.

'Well, I got to the point where I realised that my ceiling in mountain biking was not going to let me go anywhere with it. I had more potential to do something with triathlon.'

The transition came naturally. Lewis and Ruby were good cross-country runners and

so swimming was the only missing link. They learnt to swim in the lake below the house.

'I remember my first Xterra, which was my first triathlon ever,' Lewis recalls. 'That first one I did with Dad. We got this surfing wetsuit that we borrowed off a neighbour and we did four swims to the rock and back before the race. So I knew I could swim one kilometre and be able to make it through the swim.'

In the race, Brendan and Lewis started way out to the left where there was no one, in order to avoid 'the kerfuffle of all the people'.

'We came out of the water and we must've been near the back,' Lewis says. 'I wasn't much of a swimmer.'

Lewis took a long time in transition as he got out of his wetsuit, dried himself off and put on his cycling shoes.

'This was at the time when we were mountain-bike racing,' he clarifies. 'So we rode our way through most people and somehow ended up near the front. We then ran and walked the ten kilometres and somehow did very well.'

That result meant he was on his way to represent New Zealand at the Xterra World Champs, which he did in 2014, in Maui, Hawai'i. It was his second-ever triathlon and he finished third in the world for his age group.

'Maui is one of the hardest races. It'll break some of the best people in the world. I remember just going to do it completely oblivious,' he says. 'I was standing up at the ceremony as they call out the oldest competitor and there's some ninety-year-old dude and then they call out the youngest competitor and it happened to be me.'

Lewis fell in love with the sport through his experience in Maui. That soon transitioned into falling in love with always trying to be better — to try and find better in everything he did.

'That's probably more the obsession that has grown inside me,' he says. 'I have absolute

love for the sport, but I've really fallen in love
with that goal to always try to be better.'

He said his biggest achievement came in
September 2018 when he won his first pro
race on the Xterra World Tour.

'My dream was to be good enough to turn
professional. Then to be racing with the
heroes of the sport. And then the goal from
that is naturally to try and beat them in a
race. That happened for me in Taiwan.

'The guy who was second, Ben Allen, is an
absolute legend of the sport,' Lewis explains.
'He is an incredible athlete, and he was one
of the guys I looked up to most — even when I
started racing. You tick off one milestone and
then you move to the next one. They all have a
special place in your heart because of different
reasons.'

In Taiwan, Lewis was nursing an injury
that luckily never flared up. He wanted to go
back and try to win again.

'I trained incredibly hard to put myself in a
position to do that,' he admits. 'And then I got
injured. I ruptured my IT band. It was the first
time in my life that I'd really had an injury.
I've never broken a bone — up until that point
life had been pretty smooth.'

An iliotibial band rupture is a common
injury for long-distance runners. Lewis was
instantly surrounded by professionals and
people trying to help him.

'The reality is that it didn't work,' Lewis
sighs. 'My mind fell out of the game a little
bit.'

That came at a time when Lewis was
growing, and life was evolving.

'Suné and I ended up moving to Auckland
for jobs, and that's been a really exciting
chapter in my life as well,' he explains. 'Suné
and I have shared some huge triumphs, like
Taiwan, and then she's been right there to
see the lows of not performing and trying to

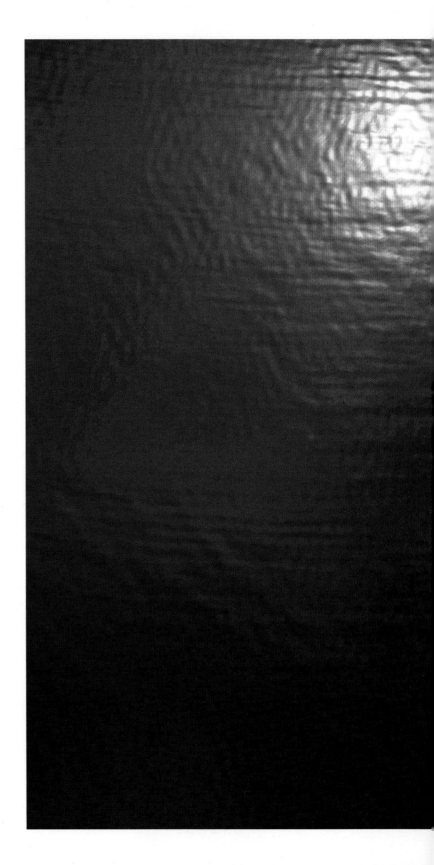

deal with injury for the first time.'

Lewis said that he had realised through it all that he has a 'burning passion and desire to race and to reach his unfulfilled potential there'.

'That desire to be better is what gets me out of the bed in the morning and what makes me want to do better all the time,' he says.

Together with Suné, Lewis runs a successful content-production company out of Auckland: We Dare.

I'm secretly glad he didn't become a chef — the geothermally cooked beans are lukewarm. But the mission was worth it.

—

Lewis took his success and learnings as an athlete and passed them directly on to his younger sister. When he made the Rotorua mountain-biking squad at 11, she did, too.

'I was coached by Lewis from twelve until I was seventeen,' Ruby says. 'That was really cool. I did a lot of riding with Lewis after school — we rode together all the time. That is my favourite thing about mountain biking; that it brought me and Lewis so close.'

Lewis tells me I wouldn't believe how many moments they've shared out there. Particularly when he was coaching her to jump a gap or try a technical section of trail.

'I swear, half the time he's tried to kill me,' she laughs. 'He's always like, "No, I promise you can do it."'

She says that relationship has developed her into being at the level she is now.

'We've just always been riding and always training,' Ruby explains. 'Training is just my life — it always has been. It's not a chore for me.'

When I sat down with the Ryan family, it was late 2019 — before Covid. Ruby had just

turned 18 and had returned from the 2019 World Mountain Bike Championships and her first season racing internationally. It had been a busy year. She had competed in six Junior World Series races on top of the New Zealand season, and then the World Champs.

'It has been my highlight year, really,' she says. 'I've had such a cool year. I won my first Junior World Series race in Japan and every Junior World Series race that I did, I podiumed at.'

Three days before flying out for her World Championship campaign, she had a training crash off a jump. She was concussed and chipped her tooth.

'I was so sick with concussion that we weren't going to go,' Ruby explains. 'I was bed-bound for three days, just completely out of it. But I was not going to miss it. For two weeks, I didn't do one whole training ride up until my race. I just had to do nothing. It was my first World Champs, so I wasn't expecting much.'

Ruby said she was at the age where most female New Zealand mountain-biking athletes dropped out. The sport became too hard and other avenues, university or work, beckoned.

'Cross-country is too hard for people, to be honest,' she tells me. 'It's such a tough sport. I've had to make some decisions, but I'm definitely sticking with it, because there's no real point in training for eighteen years to not do more. That's what I want to do.'

—

Later, over dinner, Lewis and Ruby start to debate their philosophies in sport. It's intriguing to witness and intrinsically linked to their childhood.

'We are competitive, but we naturally try to do a little bit better at everything — it's in

A bush track leads to their jetty on the lake.

our culture,' Lewis begins. 'Even when we are playing, abseiling out of our tree hut, we are trying to be the best we can.'

Ruby admits that everyone does sport for fun, but she found fun in being better at it.

'Our parents never pushed us, but they've always empowered us to do what we wanted to do, and they've motivated us at the times when we have needed motivation,' Lewis says. 'As a kid, there are plenty of times when you're growing up and you might take it the wrong way. But I think what you're really getting from this is the staying power. You can learn to hang in there — that's really what training in sport is; you're really just hanging in there. There's nothing fun about crying yourself to sleep over not performing.'

Ruby nods her head and adds, 'There is nothing fun about the idea of it. But when we are doing it, we actually quite like it. I love the pain when I'm doing it.'

Lewis says he often wondered what he and Ruby had put their parents through.

'It must be tough having teenagers at the best of times, then to have teenagers who think they're the best athletes in the world? Teenagers who are tired and focused on themselves. We must have put them through some shit. I really hope we didn't.'

THE SEA CHANGE SURFERS

THE KLEIN OVINK FAMILY —

PAPAMOA, TAURANGA

Many people dream of shaking off the shackles of city life and moving to the beach, but very few actually do it. It's a big risk. Financially, it can be disastrous. But for the Klein Ovink family, the financial risk couldn't match the lifestyle benefits on their holistic balance sheet. They've just moved to Papamoa.

The Klein Ovinks are a family of surfers. They first started their surf adventures five years ago, but already Kelly and Richard's 19-year-old daughter Baylin, 17-year-old son Isaac and 13-year-old son PJ are competing in the country's toughest surf competitions.

They're natural sportspeople, with the benefit of two parents who coach businesses on how to use mindset and culture to realise peak performance.

Learning to surf based on the wave-starved coastline of Maraetai in Auckland's

southeastern corner was always going to
prove to be a challenge.

'We'd go to Port Waikato or Karioitahi,'
Kelly tells me. 'It was an hour and a quarter to
our nearest surf spot, if there was no traffic.'

Kelly's parents own a place in Pāuanui,
so that would become a regular weekend
destination for surfing. About three years
ago, the kids turned their attention towards
competitive surfing.

'They used to play soccer all winter,'
Richard explains. 'And we said, "Hey guys,
if you wanted to give up soccer, we could go
every weekend and find surf somewhere."
And from there it just took on a life of its own.'

The surf competitions were a whole new
world. At that stage, they had never belonged

to a boardriders club and Maraetai did not
have a lot of surfers.

'We would email the school and take
Fridays off,' Kelly remembers. 'We had to take
time off to travel to the surf comps — it was
always a long way from there. I don't know
how many Fridays they did at school.'

'This past year, I've done maybe five
Fridays at school,' smiles Isaac, quite happy
with the stat.

Richard, who is 44, tells me that they have
never pushed the kids into surfing.

'It's been motivated and driven by them,'
he says. 'For us, it's fun first. It's the healthy
side of what surfing is.'

That was particularly hard at first, when
they would travel long distances and the kids

PREVIOUS SPREAD
Baylin Klein Ovink
(centre) waits for a set
to arrive with her dad
Richard and mum Kelly.

ABOVE
The Klein Ovink family
(from left): Isaac, PJ,
Baylin, Cruz, Kelly and
Richard.

OPPOSITE
Moving-in week
coincides with finishing-
the-house-off week.

would get knocked out of the contest in their first heat.

'You're just like, "Oh, we've driven all this way for a fifteen-minute surf,"' Kelly smiles. 'And then I'd sit there and think, *We can just go to any beach and surf for four hours. Why are we doing this?* Then I realised if they wanted to keep doing it, we'd have to find the other good parts of it all. Once we got the campervan and connected with all the surfing families, I realised this is actually amazing. In the middle of building a house, would you go to Kaikōura? Of course, you wouldn't. But because of that event, it made us stop, prioritise family, jump in the camper and do the trip. It's perfect.'

Baylin and her brothers now have a network of friends right throughout New Zealand because of surfing.

'I love watching the kids on the sideline,' Kelly adds. 'You watch kids spend an entire day at the beach with no toys, no devices, but they just entertain themselves. They hang out and play with sticks, smoky campfires. I think that's so healthy.'

She admits that as they've progressed, they've learnt how to surf for a comp.

'It is different, as we've found out,' Kelly explains. 'It's actually a lot of strategy. And about being consistent.'

Kelly is 42 now and she and Richard both surf, although they are latecomers to the sport. Richard was 35 when he gave it a decent nudge.

'The kids were old enough to have little foamy boards,' he says. 'So, as they learnt to surf, I learnt to surf.'

Kelly was on the beach 'pretending to watch them' and getting bored.

'So they got me a Mother's Day board and I loved it.' She hasn't looked back.

Richard said they loved surfing together as a family and the sport side of it all.

'I've been involved in heaps of sports: football, golf, rugby, squash, tennis and heaps of others, and this is the best sport by a long shot,' he says. 'We still snowboard, because we like it a lot. And we do bit of golf when there are no waves.'

I ask them jokingly who's the best surfer among them.

PJ is quick to respond: 'Probably Isaac.'

They say that they are all better than their mum and dad.

'There's no question,' laughs Kelly. 'I'm always like, "Well, what can I work on next, kids?" They always say, "Your pop-up still, Mum."'

—

With Kelly's extended family living near their home in Maraetai, their business tapping into the city and the kids settled at school, Kelly and Richard were locked into the area. But as the kids grew older, their priorities started to change.

'We started to think of other options,'

ABOVE
Isaac is one of
New Zealand's top
competitive surfers,
making the most here of
a wave at Pony Club.

OPPOSITE
(Clockwise from left)
Furniture layout in a
blank canvas.

Moving-in day at the
Klein Ovinks' new
Papamoa home.

Pony Club is the new
local surf sport for the
Klein Ovink family.

The surf is just a hop,
skip and a jump from
their new home.

Richard says. 'Baylin had gone to the Raglan
Surf Academy for Year 13, which was an
amazing opportunity.'

'It was my final year of school and it was
epic,' Baylin adds. 'It definitely improved my
surfing. You're in a cool crew — all very good
surfers, and it pushes you. You surf every day
and train three days a week before school, and
then Tuesday mornings we have heats, and
then you surf again in the afternoon. When
it's daylight savings, you'll surf with them,
then you'll talk about it with the coaches and
go back out before dark.'

Once Baylin had completed the academy
at Raglan, she'd been exposed to a different
way of life — a life by the surf coast. Kelly
and Richard were already sniffing around to
see what properties were available around
Papamoa.

'She was like "I'm not coming back to
Auckland,"' Kelly remembers. 'Then Isaac
was like, "Sign me up for Raglan", because
he wanted to get out. We didn't really
imagine having no kids with us. We wanted
to do the teenage years. And then we were
like, "Well, why are we staying? We want to
surf, too."'

—

The timing of my first visit to their home
coincides with moving-in week. Richard is
rushing to finish the stairwell and all the kids
have tasks. They've been immersed in the

build, as a family, and they're kind of wrecked when I arrive.

The house is modest but beautiful — an expansive family dwelling. From the top floor, you can catch glimpses of the waves — 'when they're over five foot', PJ tells me as he trains his binos on the dune crest. It has five bedrooms, two big living spaces and they're about to add in a board room and outdoor shower area.

There are boxes everywhere, and the section carries the hallmarks of a big building project with pallets and materials scattered here and there.

They bought the section in October 2019 and sold in Auckland around the same time.

'We had decided we wanted to come

towards the Papamoa end rather than the Mount, which is quite busy,' Kelly says. 'We both grew up on farms, so we were keener on a quieter spot. We were looking at a map and we put a circle around where we would like to be. We'd just done a massive clean getting our house in Auckland ready to sell, and we sat down at the end of one day and I said to Richard, "Look, there's a section for sale." It was right here among all these houses and it was a private sale. It was a bit of a miracle.'

'We hadn't even stood on it when we bought it,' smiles Richard.

Their work allows them some degree of flexibility.

'We travel a little bit up and down, and Covid has been a bit of a slow-down,' Richard

says. 'But we already had a couple of clients down here. And we've picked up some more, and we'll pick up others. As the kids get older, we'll be quite comfortable to drive up and stay somewhere for a couple of nights to do some work.'

Kelly and Richard run a company called Populus, which delivers business-skills training to businesses large and small.

'We work a lot around performance and culture,' Richard explains. 'We help their people to be better at what they do, whether it is sales or leadership management, which then contributes to culture as well.'

Kelly said they kept their team small to protect the quality of the training.

'We do this because, one, we love it, and, two, it's lifestyle for us,' Richard says. 'Freedom, and flexibility, are important to us.'

'We were always fighting for that balance,' adds Kelly. 'It's funny to talk about living the dream, because we're actually living the dream.'

Richard describes the hard work to get there as being like a 'season in life'.

'You set out your goals,' says Kelly. 'And the goal is freaking hard work. But you're doing it because you know what it will mean in the end.'

They have tried to instil that work ethic in the kids.

'Even with the move and the build, we told them: "We need you all on board. You can't just turn up when your house looks amazing and your room's all set up,"' Kelly says. 'The hard part is the part that counts.'

Isaac said it was nice to see every step of the build.

'I've learnt a lot, watching and helping Dad throughout this process. It's cool to see it come together.'

Baylin tells me they actually did 'lots of it'.

OPPOSITE
The family relax after an early surf — they like to prioritise quality time together.

ABOVE
Breakfast time at the Klein Ovinks'.

Cruz, just cruising.

'We did all the insulation, all the wiring. I helped the electrician for three or four weeks.'

Isaac laid tiles with his dad and his grandad, while PJ put the door handles in and chiselled out all the door jambs.

One of the goals for the kids is to get across to one of the area's premium surf spots, The Island, across the harbour entrance from the Mount. They even bought a boat for the trip, but Richard and Kelly have made them wait until the house is finished.

'The kids keep saying, "Let's go to The Island,"' he laughs. 'I tell them, "Let's finish the house first."'

Isaac surfs with his good friend Jack Hinton when he can, and has been to The Island two or three times 'when it was small'.

'It actually gets pretty fun right out here in front,' Isaac tells me. 'We have a wave out here called Pony Club, which used to be called Gravel Pits, and another wave directly out the front of our house as well.'

PJ surfs a lot with other top New Zealand surfers and locals Tao Mouldey and Tyler Stenzel.

'Tyler lives just down the road. He is home-schooled as well,' PJ says. 'I go to the skateboard bowl with them, and we surf together.'

PJ is schooled through Te Kura and has taken to it superbly.

'I've got a teacher and we meet online every two weeks,' he explains. 'We email back and forth, similar to what everyone did in lockdown. I have two websites for maths and stuff that I do — modules — and I do all these different subjects online. I get up early in the morning and I'm done by eleven, and then we just go surfing.'

Richard said the recommendation for home-school was somewhere between three and four hours each day.

ABOVE
Motorhome life as the kids follow the surfing circuit around the country.

OPPOSITE
Richard hasn't been surfing long, but he is determined to keep up with his kids.

'He does that generally and his schoolwork has improved,' Richard says. 'His reading has improved. His baking has improved — he can cook. When he comes to help with building the house, he can put that as part of his learning. So it's quite cool; it's nice and holistic. PJ has got the right personality for it.'

'It's real life,' adds Kelly. 'And the self-management that he has had to figure out is great.'

Isaac is not so sure he likes the new regime.

'I'll come back from school and he will have just got in and tells me he's had a great surf,' he laughs. 'I get frustrated.'

They've seen orca out the front and, not too long ago, PJ and Tao got to surf with dolphins.

'That was cool,' he smiles. 'It was tiny and we just went out anyway. Tao was talking about sharks and then, he was like, "There's dolphins." They were swimming under us and everything. And we see heaps of stingrays, too. I saw like fifty in one surf once.'

Baylin starts chuckling as she remembers an occasion when they were surfing at Whakatāne and the shallows were teeming with stingrays.

'Mum was yelling at the boys, "Boys, we have to form a single-file line,"' she laughs.

'I just thought if we go in a line, at least we're not shooing them into each other,' Kelly says. 'There were so many. You couldn't even put a foot down. It was awful.'

—

Surfing quickly took over their lives and even prescribed the type of people they could socialise with.

'Surf friends understand that you can say, "Yes, we're going to have dinner, but it could be an early dinner, or a really late dinner." Or maybe we won't even eat dinner because we're so late in the water,' laughs Kelly. 'If the surf's good, no one wants to commit.'

That is why they enjoy spending Christmas in Pāuanui with friends Matt and Amber Groube, who are in the same position.

'It's just so easy because we're all like, "Sweet, we'll all go surf, and then eat and then surf again." Everyone understands.'

—

Early one morning in summer, a few months after they'd moved into their new home, I meet the family at their gate. A tropical cyclone swell has arrived. We cross the road before the sun comes up and paddle out into the murky darkness. The crack and boom of the swell guides us to the take-off point.

For three hours, they surf rings around each other, hoot, laugh and smile. It's a pretty magical experience, and they're together as a family for it.

Afterwards, Kelly and Richard tell me they have always encouraged their kids to remain open to growth, change and moving forward.

Baylin was planning to take a gap year and travel before Covid ruined her plans. She did a stint working in Pāuanui with Matt Groube

ABOVE
The line-up outside their new home springs to life with a cyclone swell.

OPPOSITE
Baylin attended the Raglan Surf Academy for her final year of school.

Kelly takes off on a set wave during a cyclone swell.

PJ makes the most of a dawn session at Pony Club.

in his tree business there.

'He's so busy. We would smash out ten to twelve decent-sized jobs a day and he would've taken on like eight new jobs,' she remembers. 'He only really checked four off the list. Some days, I was dying feeding the chipper. His dad is eighty-two and he's still doing it. I'm like, "How are you still going?" I asked him one day: "Are you ever going to stop?" He told me: "No, I'm going to keep doing this until one day I'm going to cut a pine tree and it's going to fall on top of me, and it's going to be like, 'Finally got you, you bugger!'"'

Baylin worked in a café for a bit, before helping with the build. Now she's looking at doing an electrical apprenticeship.

'A family friend was wiring up this house so I was just like, *Okay, I might as well learn*,' she explains. She ran all the wires for their new home.

'She realised that she enjoyed that more than digging trenches and all the plumbing jobs,' Kelly laughs.

School had been hard for Isaac, so Kelly and Richard said he could leave once he completed Year 12. Isaac tells me he's now going to make money, and surf.

'I don't know how yet,' he admits.

Isaac has a lot of ideas 'and a grandfather who is very entrepreneurial and might influence him', Richard says.

'He was going to have a caravan selling crêpes, restore old furniture; he was going to breed sausage dogs . . . so just exploring ideas at this stage,' smiles Kelly.

While they don't go to church, they are involved in the Christian surfers community. Isaac and Baylin help to run a regular grom night, where they take kids skating and surfing. Community is important to Richard and Kelly, and they help out wherever they can.

'We love what we do. We love people,' Kelly smiles. 'We don't ever think about retiring. There's no end goal. We don't want to have a career, earn all this money and then say, "Oh, hey guys, we're available because we've got this money now." Then they'll be eighteen and won't want to hang out with us as much. That time doesn't come back.'

'We've been very intentional about the decisions that we've made along those lines,' Richard adds.

'We might not have the coolest everything, but I don't feel like we miss out,' Kelly says. 'The experiences, and the people you meet along the way — that is the point.'

ABOVE
Isaac surfs even on the flat days, but lives for each new swell.

OPPOSITE
PJ and Isaac's lives have changed for good in Papamoa.

THE SALTWATER MONK

DAVE TIMBS — WAINUI BEACH,

GISBORNE

'It's like the bonnet of an old Vauxhall,' Dave tells me as he drops into a chair on his porch. 'You know, when you're sitting in those old cars and they've got this bonnet that drops away in front of you — well, this is my version of that.'

He's proud of his lawn. It's featureless apart from a picnic table and a set of stairs in one corner. The stairs lead to Wainui Beach and its bounty of waves beyond, and this is what first drew Dave Timbs to Gisborne back in 1972.

His home is one of the original baches along the beachfront — it's becoming a rarity as Wainui develops and grows into an increasingly affluent suburb. Large, sprawling houses are engulfing the classic Kiwi asbestos-laden baches that once defined this stretch of coastline. But not at Dave's place.

He reads the water in front of us like a well-

loved map: 'We have Stock Route to the right. And then Cooper Street down further, which has its own peaks at times. Then there's No Access to the left, and then Schools along a bit further.'

Each peak has its own name and character, but he throws a canvas over the whole lot: 'This is the iconic Wainui Beach.' Dave has been surfing for more than 60 years.

When Dave stumbled across the bach for sale 20 years ago, it seemed nobody wanted it. He offered $190,000 and landed on his feet. Apart from adding a porch on either end to 'enhance the indoor—outdoor flow', and a few other adaptions, he's barely changed a thing.

'I wake up every morning and never take it for granted. I really appreciate it,' he smiles.

PREVIOUS SPREAD
Dave and partner Mel take in the dusk from their porch on the beachfront at Wainui.

OPPOSITE
Boards ready to go on the lawn.

Dawn reveals a new swell.

ABOVE
(Clockwise from left) Waves peak up in front of Dave's lawn.

Dave stands with a board shaped by friend and iconic artist and shaper Daryn McBride. The artwork shows Dave's little house through the tube of a wave at Cooper Street.

The beach-style kitchen.

'As a surfer, you just want to be able to go and look out at the surf and, somehow, I landed here and I've done it. Nobody wanted to even live at Wainui Beach back then.'

Since he bought his bach, the real estate in Wainui has steadily become premium. Wealthy purchasers have fuelled the rising prices and inadvertently changed the culture of the place in the process.

'I don't hold it against them or think that it's affluence gone wrong,' Dave says. 'But with sea levels rising, beachfronts being threatened and the government talking about managed retreat, it is going to be interesting to see how people who have built these larger houses deal with that.'

He says they'll try to fight it, but he was happy to sit and just watch it go on around him within his lifetime.

'It does also mean that we no longer know the community,' he adds. 'We used to know everybody and would almost be able to walk into any house and say hello. That's completely changed. But there are still young families, people who have maybe sold a couple of houses to buy or build their dream home.'

—

Dave was born and raised in Tītahi Bay near Wellington. His father was one of the area's founding fathers and helped establish a lot of the institutions within the bay, including getting phone lines installed. His father

helped build their house on the beachfront at Tītahi Bay — right in front of where the surf was.

'It was just a natural thing to engage with the ocean,' Dave says. 'My brother was older than me and we had to teach ourselves because there were no movies, there were no magazines, there were no photographs back then.'

Dave was about eight at the time — around 1959. They had no idea what other people were doing around the world.

'I can clearly remember sitting after a surf saying, "I'm sure you can walk on these boards — instead of shuffling, we will try walking,"' he recalls. 'So, we'd got out there as kids and we'd take a few steps, fall off, swim

in. We taught ourselves to walk the board.'

Later on, they discovered that everybody was doing that.

'It was like the hundredth monkey thing, where if the monkeys on one island start to use tools, and there are enough of them using tools, then all of a sudden the monkeys on the neighbouring island start using tools. Surfing was a bit like that.

'It was a great life. We would surf in Wellington the whole year round without wetsuits, because there weren't any wetsuits. You couldn't buy a wetsuit back then. It was rugby jerseys and old woollen singlets.'

In the beginning, they were surfing very basic 'paipo boards' that their father made for them.

Wainui is home to Dave, though he doesn't dare call himself a local.

'They were little wooden things that would cut you in half because they were flat and they'd pearl and you'd get stabbed in the gut and flipped over,' he laughs, showing me the action. 'You'd come in with big red marks around your gut from when you got hammered.'

As surfing evolved, Dave kept pace. An old friend who grew up over the road worked for Atlas Woods and secured Dave sponsorship with the board manufacturer.

'I was not a competitive surfer but I was Wellington Junior Champ,' he tells me. 'And ended up Wellington Senior Champ one year, too.'

He only surfed in the National Surfing Championships once.

'I went to New Plymouth on my five-foot-six twin-fin Atlas Woods, with no leg rope, and I got absolutely smashed at Stent Road in my heat,' he recalls. 'And that was it for me. I was out the back door. I went straight back to Wellington and got a mate to shape a board that was moulded on Alan Byrne's, who had won the nationals. We were on the wrong equipment. This little twin-fin was all right for Tītahi Bay onshores, but not for Kūmara Patch or Stent Road.'

It was in Tītahi Bay and through surfing that he became friends with poet and entertainer Gary McCormick.

'He lived in the same street and we were the best of surf mates,' Dave explains. 'We used to surf a lot together, and he'd wake me

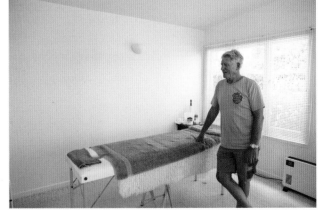

up in the morning. He'd come to our two-storey house and he'd throw little stones up at the window and I'd hear this *tink, tink, tink* on the window and I'd know he would want to go for a surf before school.'

Dave was brought up getting blasted by the onshores at Tītahi Bay. The nor'wester would smash the family house and cover it with salt spray. He always thought the east coast was gentler. He knew Gisborne produced good surfers and had heard about the surf there. In 1972, aged 21, he made a beeline for Poverty Bay.

'I moved here to be a teacher, but it was really to come surfing,' he smiles. 'It was a pretty revolutionary time of the hippy era — establishing new boundaries and new rules.'

ABOVE
Sunshine fills Dave's treatment room in the back garden. His practice includes numerous holistic medicinal approaches.

He said they struggled with the teaching culture. The old establishment was still in charge, and they were long-haired hippies who had come out of teachers' college full of ideas.

'We weren't really embraced,' Dave says. 'We were told to shape up or ship out. A lot of the guys who I trained with shipped out. I didn't last long. Teaching in a state school was a terrible job.'

Alongside his teaching and travelling, Dave was following his interest in natural healthcare. He accumulated qualifications and experience as he explored his passion. It was never his intention to become a practitioner, but he wanted to share what he'd learnt.

'I started to share it by opening up a clinic in 1980,' he explains. 'And that's been part of my life ever since.'

He also created some adult-education courses for long-term unemployed that the government funded. They weaved in all of his natural healthcare interests and skills, from organic gardening to vegetarian cooking, to nutrition and massage, herbs and all the natural therapies and Ayurveda, or Indian medicine.

'I'd do two of those a year. They were six months long, and I had that going for ten years. That got me on my feet and running my clinic at the same time. I was teaching from nine until three and then running the clinic from three till six. That allowed me to buy this house.'

He says it never felt like work to him.

'I was never a smart cookie, so I never thought that I had any special head start at all. I did about fourteen years of part- or full-time education after I left school. And I left school with what I would class as not being able to read. I trained as a teacher, but I had to teach myself to read during that year when I was first teaching — I faked it and bluffed it. I found things that I was interested in, then I

had to learn to study, and I enjoyed it.'

He admits he had no idea what the outcome was going to be at the time. He certainly didn't expect it to lead to a lifelong profession.

'It was a lifestyle,' Dave tells me. 'I lived what I learnt. It was not until I could integrate some of the knowledge into my life that I was prepared to go to the next step and learn more.'

He has weaved parts of his learning into everything he does and represents.

'I've had this philosophy that if you spend your whole life getting rid of what you're not, then it's a life well spent. There was nothing wrong with my upbringing, or my education. I was never instilled with a religious philosophy that can control my life. I had a lot of freedom anyway, but it was really about getting rid of all the things which you feel aren't you and then seeing what's left. Peeling back the layers of the onion. If it's not working, then there's no point in hanging on to it — it doesn't matter what it is. Whether it is a spiritual philosophy, or practice, or an occupation.'

Dave was born into a family that had, for 200 years, produced butchers through the sons in his father's line. His father told him supermarkets would kill the trade and discouraged him from that path. This was partially a relief for Dave, who had different ideas about the butchery trade.

'I changed my diet and I was all about nature and connecting with the earth and all of that,' he explains. 'That is why I studied naturopathy and Ayurveda, the Indian philosophy, which means "the science of life". I'm still fascinated by that and I've been interested in it for thirty years.'

Dave was initiated into a meditative practice in 1975, one which was from an Eastern philosophy — not Buddhism, but he says he'd always appreciated the way that modern Western Buddhism doesn't judge people.

'That allows people to become the best version of themselves that they can,' he says. 'It is also about not leaving too much of a footprint behind — it doesn't matter what it is. I really respect that version of a philosophy to live by. Every system has its downsides or the people who maybe don't practise it one hundred per cent. So, I don't judge any philosophy by the individuals.'

—

My 11-year-old son Keo has joined me on this trip and takes the opportunity to go surfing while Dave makes another pot of coffee. It's the perfect location — we can see him paddling around the peaks directly in front of the house. Dave tells me he turned 70 in January and that marks 40 years of meditative practice for him.

'I don't think it's been the be all and end all,' he admits. 'It's a nice thing to have in your armoury. I always have a happy place to go to in my mind. I always say, "You wake up to your mind, so make it your friend." My mind is always my friend. It's never an enemy that is turning against me or feels as though it is out of control, or it's taken over me. I still feel I am in control of my mind rather than my mind being in control of me. And that's maybe through the meditative practice that gives you that little piece of separation of standing back from your own thoughts.'

He said these days it is all about mindfulness meditation: observing your own thinking and not buying into your thoughts.

'There is a strong relationship between surfing and meditation — a close link,' Dave says. 'One of the hooks in surfing that a lot of people don't see is that when you're surfing, you're often not thinking. Your best waves are the ones that, when you flick off, felt really good, but you can't even recall a lot of what you did on the wave. It just felt really good.

'It is a non-thinking state,' he continues.

'If you're teaching people to surf, you don't put them on the beach and give them all these instructions — you'll be training them to think. As soon as you think in surfing, it's all over, it's gone. It's got to be a non-thinking state. It has to be a reflex and a feel.'

He says that's what the meditative practice is training you to do.

'When we think: one, two, three, four, or one apple, one tree, one coffee, one horse, between one and the next word, there's a gap,' he explains. 'Well, that's where that word comes from. It comes out of that gap, and our memory is in that gap. So that gap is actually more important than the thought, and yet all our education is based on the thought.

'When you're surfing, you're accessing that gap a little bit,' he tells me. 'When Keo is out there, he's surfing in the cold water. He's paddling around, exercising. He's doing plunges under the cold, cold water. If you tell an eleven-year-old kid, "I want you to go out in cold water and dive under the water and paddle around exercising", they'll go, "Forget it. What the hell am I going to do that for?" But then you get them to ride a wave and they go: "I'm hooked. Hey, Dad, can I go surfing?" There's something that happens when they're riding the wave.'

Dave says people often misunderstand the dynamic of a wave. Specifically, that the water is not moving laterally — the water is only going up and down.

'The only thing that's moving is an energy,' he explains. 'Until the wave breaks, the water is not moving. So, not only is Keo getting into a non-thinking state, but he's actually getting to ride energy. And there's not many places on the planet where you get to ride an energy wave.

'People who surf can match it with somebody who's been three years in a cave in the Himalayas, trying to get into these non-thinking states,' he smiles. 'And kids get it really early in life and they get it almost

Dave and his partner, Mel, dressed for date night on a Friday evening.

instantly. It's like you've fast-forwarded your experience of being a monk in the Himalayas. Fast-forwarded it by thirty years. That becomes the drug. It's not all a culture of what company you're surfing for and sponsorship and everything else. It's actually that moment of non-thinking and riding an energy wave.'

In the back garden, Dave has a small building where he sees his clients. He has photos on the wall of people who have touched his life. There's Miki Dora; 2001 World Junior Surfing Champion and Wainui boy Jay Quinn; his 34-year-old son Robson and 37-year-old daughter Darnelle (a 2004 World Rowing Champion); and his old mate, Gary McCormick.

His clients come from all walks of life:

fencers, forestry workers and people who wake up in pain and want to be fixed instantly.

'I try to fix people in one session because people don't want to come back over and over again,' Dave tells me. 'If you don't have that intention, then you're not going to have that outcome; that's why I don't work with ACC. I work on a koha basis and I say, "You put your koha in the box. What you think is a fair price, but don't tell me what it is." If I'm no good at my job, then people aren't going to come.'

—

Dave's son Robson joins us after surfing some dreamy waves right in front of the lawn. He's a talented surfer. He pulls up a chair as Dave recounts one of his travel adventures: living in a tent for two months on a beach at Rio Nexpa in Mexico.

'It had this big left-hand point break,' he begins, his eyes widening at the memory. 'At first, I wouldn't paddle out to the end of the point. It was just too big and I remember looking down the face, thinking, *Holy shit, do I want to go down there?* But after a couple of months, I was just into it.'

When he first arrived there, he didn't have a board or even a tent.

'I ended up having a board every day and I never asked for one once,' he smiles. 'I arrived and a guy was leaving — he had injured his back. So I gave his back a bit of a click and he gave me his tent. I lived on ten bucks a day all up, for everything. I had to pay two dollars a day to put my tent on the beach. And then I just lived on mangoes and avocados. There was a restaurant up on poles there and I offered to give them a hand, because it was a family-run thing. They couldn't pay me, so once a week I'd get a meal and that was my only meal. It was mangoes and avocados, seven days a week, other than that one meal.'

Robson leans forward and probes a little more: 'How old were you when you did that, Dad?'

It turns out Dave was 60 when he took that trip. Some 40 years earlier, he was lucky to return home alive from one of his adventures.

At 22, he started travelling and decided to embark on a yacht trip.

'We were sailing a trimaran to Tonga and we got whacked by a cyclone,' he says. 'We got these huge waves, three times the size of the boat, and I thought I was dead. We were surfing down the face of waves at twenty-one knots in this trimaran, which would get up and plane and then bury the hulls in the trough of the wave up to the cabin. I thought, *Oh, this is it — we're gonna flip or roll.*'

Each time, the boat would come up and off they'd go again.

Dave was one of three crew, and they ended up spending a week out at sea. It was the last 24 hours that nearly got them.

'We were hove to,' he remembers. 'We had everything tied down and the boat just steered itself. I heard this noise that sounded like a train coming. This wave hit the front of the boat, knocked the window out and flooded the chart table. The whole front of the boat was full of water.'

It was about 5.30 a.m. and Dave was down in the front half of the boat, up to his waist in water, pumping it out, while the skipper, Roy, tried to seal the window. Jan, the other person who was on the voyage, tried to steer the boat to keep them going with the waves.

'That was the start of a hell twenty-four hours,' Dave says, shaking his head. 'It just got bigger and bigger. I've always been around the ocean and I tried to imagine the worst that the ocean could get, and it got that bad and then worse again. The whole ocean was mountain, trough, mountain, trough. Our wind gauge only went up to sixty knots and it went off the top of that. It was picking up the tops of the wave and just blowing them to the crest of the next wave. We'd never know when we would get a broken wave roll over us. I thought I was dead.'

Dave was on deck from 5.30 a.m. until 7 a.m. the next day.

'The agreement was if you washed overboard, you were dead,' he adds. 'There was one point where Roy was having to change the headsail to a storm jib and I had to pull it up and put the mainsheet on, but a wave came across the side and he had to wrap his arms around the stainless-steel railings at the front. The wave went over him. I was waiting to see if he was still there when the wave went by. Luckily, he popped out. I had to get this rope tied up and get it winched in with wind in the sail to get the boat to straighten

out before the next wave came across, otherwise we were going to be toast.'

But that wasn't the only close shave Dave would have. About six years ago, Dave was surfing down by Schools when he started to feel a little pain in his chest. He thought it was rib pain and carried on surfing. Robson had arrived back from Aussie the day before and was standing on the edge of the lawn as Dave approached. Robson insisted he went to the hospital.

Dave had experienced two cardiac arrests. He was flown to Hamilton for an angiogram, and the doctors removed a clot and put a stent in. Last year, he went and did a routine stress test, which showed something wasn't right. He returned to Hamilton for another angiogram. That showed tissue had grown through the stent and partially blocked it off. He was able to get it cleared.

'Dying twice and coming out of it unscathed was a great experience,' he says. 'It's not one that you usually have in life. It's like going to a hidden temple somewhere that's really hard to get to. And you're lucky if you come out alive, but I did. I went there, I experienced it and I lived to tell the tale. About a week afterwards, I was sitting around home with both of my kids. I thought, *Oh, maybe it's just as well I didn't die because these guys would be organising my funeral right now. And that'd be a bit rough on them.* It was a bit too early for it.'

—

Dave has a couple of nuggets of wisdom that he has learnt from his 70 years on the planet, and the first is 'not to shit on anybody'.

'In your lifetime, you can actually just be a nice person,' he says. 'And it takes just as much effort to be happy as it does to be sad. So you might as well just put that effort into being happy.'

Dave says the best decisions he has made in

OPPOSITE
Surfing is a kind of meditation for Dave.

At 70, Dave has no intention to stop surfing.

Dave's son Robson glides along in front of the home he grew up in.

NEXT SPREAD
Dave's home is one of few remaining original baches at Wainui.

his life have been the spontaneous ones.

'My kids say I'm like a cat,' he smiles. 'Every time you drop a cat, it lands on its feet. My life's a bit like that at times — if somebody dropped me, I'd land on my feet. If somebody pulls the carpet out from under me, I land on my feet, and that's not through smarts and it's not through being selfish. There's an aspect of not reacting to everything, but just acting, so you aren't being led by all the factors that are going on around you. You're listening to others to see what their points of view are, but not necessarily following them.'

—

Dave returned from his overseas travels as a very idealistic man. He lusted for adventure and found it in self-employment and marriage. After nine years, the marriage 'didn't really work out'.

He tried to give the children the view that life didn't need to be stressful and that you could actually enjoy yourself.

'I'd always try to make their life happy,' he explains. 'Every year, I'd take them on an adventure around New Zealand or somewhere to the Pacific Islands or Australia, to give them a bit of a wider view other than Gisborne being the centre of the universe.

'My philosophy was when they grow up, if I could blindfold them, put them on a plane and land them anywhere in the world, they'd get on with the locals and be able to make it home if they wanted to,' Dave says. 'To just be universal in their approach towards different cultures, different belief systems and different genders. I didn't bring them up to control them; I brought them up to set them free.'

THE MOKOTAHI
MUSTER

THE BRIDGE FAMILY —

MOKOTAHI, MĀHIA PENINSULA

Poss thought it was a brilliant idea.
We'd form a convoy and make our way from
Palmerston North to Māhia Peninsula,
chasing a promising swell. We loaded
surfboards, beer and whatever else came to
mind in the 10 minutes between the idea's
conception and our departure. We were the
bubbles in the champagne of student life in
the early 1990s.

It was a journey with a flimsy plan,
minuscule budget and no real timeframe, but
a destination that would forge a great many
friendships.

Many, many hours later, the convoy of
barely warrantable vehicles, with surfboards
haphazardly stacked on the roof, arrived at
Māhia and the Bridges' family bach. It was
dark. We knew surf conditions would be good
the next day, but Poss, with her good friend
Martha by her side, showed us how to party.

Over the next few days, we surfed some of the best waves of our lives, at places like Annihilations, Rolling Stones, Blacks Reef, Tracks, Diners and The Spit — every time by ourselves, just our group. Each night, we'd retreat to the comfort of Poss's family bach, share our surf experiences, laugh and party until we fell asleep.

University had thrown us together and we were an eclectic bunch. It still puzzles me how so many surfers ended up at Massey University that year, considering it is a minimum three hours' drive to quality waves. But, driven by a shared sense of freedom and a passion for the ocean, we thrived. We bonded in those experiences at Māhia and we laid foundations that would last a lifetime.

Poss (Melissa Bridge) left an indelible mark on all of us. That took on even more importance when our beautiful friend succumbed to her brain tumour nearly six weeks after her twenty-first birthday in September 1994.

—

Stuart Bridge was born on a farm at Te Karaka, 'way up in the back of nowhere'.

'I remember the first time Winks [Annette] and I were engaged. We drove up the Kanakanaia Road and we had Winks's parents with us,' Stu recalls. 'We stopped at the top of the hill and there's a building that looked like it was up in the heavens somewhere,

PREVIOUS SPREAD
Most of the collection of university surfing mates who have notched up almost 30 years of friendship. Gathered at Mokotahi, Māhia.

ABOVE
The township is nestled in the neck of Māhia Peninsula.

about a thousand miles away. Winks said, "Look at that building up there. I wonder who would live up there?" And I said, "Well, if you marry me, it will be you — that there is the woolshed."'

They lived there for eight years, only selling it to make schooling easier, living closer to Gisborne. That's when they bought their farm at Waerenga-o-Kuri, just 1 kilometre from school and 30 minutes to town.

Melissa was born in 1973 and Dana arrived 21 months later, and then Angus was born 19 months after Dana. Toby came four years after that in 1981.

Around 1983, Stu and Winks went for a tour around Māhia with a friend who knew everything about everyone in the place. He showed them what was for sale and what things were worth.

'On the way home, I suggested to Winks we should get her parents to come in with us — to go half-shares, because these baches were good value,' Stu says. 'We bought our first bach for $21,000, fully furnished. The person just walked out. There was even a fur coat in the drawer.'

That bach was directly behind Mokotahi, and they used to access the beach through it. It wasn't easy and they had to go to extremes to raise their half of the money.

'We made the kids go into their piggy banks — their school bank accounts,' Stu admits, shaking his head. 'We had no money, but we

managed to get our $11,000 together for our half-share and we bought that little bach.'

For various reasons, they decided to sell. It took quite a few years before it did eventually sell. When it did, Mokotahi came up.

'Winks's mother called and told us this bach was coming on the market and we said, "No, no, no — don't touch that. It's too close to the road, too public,"' Stu remembers. 'She said, "Oh, bad luck. I've already bought it — front up with your half-share."'

They paid $93,000 for what Stu describes as one of the better investments he's ever made.

Their Mokotahi purchase included the original building and a garage out the back. They soon relocated a wash house to the

site and about eight years ago they built the cabins.

'We looked locally for shearing quarters or something similar and couldn't find anything,' Winks recalls. 'I saw some lovely ones in Hawke's Bay and they were $100,000 each. Then I saw some online in Whangārei that were $5000 each, including freight.'

The cabins were designed for trout fishermen and hunters so they could fly into remote locations and have shelter.

'So we arranged to buy these things,' Winks continues. 'There are four cabins and we altered them a bit; made the veranda a bit wider and made the roof span all four. Then the day came. They were going to come down from Whangārei with them and they rang us

OPPOSITE
Stuart and Annette
Bridge love that their
Māhia bach has become
a gathering place.

ABOVE
(Clockwise from left)
The Māhia ice-cream
vendor visits Mokotahi.

All spruced up.

One of the earliest
photos of Mokotahi,
circa 1910.

Mokotahi has long been
a place where people
come together.

and said, "Right, we're on our way — what will it take us? Two hours or so?"' It took about fourteen or fifteen hours.'

Stu remembers them being 'very Mickey Mouse': nothing was square, the studs weren't at 400-millimetre centres. They were all over the place.

'I came down here with a mate and we lined them all, insulated them all, and I strengthened the roof,' he says. 'We put in more studs so we could put the ply up, and we squared everything up and redid them.'

There were downsides to owning a bach that was more than 110 years old.

'The piles go all the time,' Winks laughs. 'One Christmas, we arrived here and we couldn't open any of the cupboard doors.

Stuart could see the house had sunk. He looked under and the piles had completely rotted away. So he got the car jack and he jacked up the corner of the house to repair them.'

Replacing piles and bearers has been a constant part of owning the bach.

With the cabins in place, Mokotahi can accommodate large groups with ease. That was always part of its purpose under the Bridge family ownership — as a gathering place. They didn't realise that their children would love it so much.

'We always thought it was a good thing to do with a family,' Stu says. 'We did things as a family and played as a family. We had a lot of mates down here, too. And it's not too far from Gisborne.'

Winks and Stu would come down for the school holidays and stay the whole time. Often Stu would commute each day to work on the farm and return each evening.

'It got a bit hard, though, because a fair bit of drinking went on,' Stu confesses. 'Many late nights. I used to get up early to get home and do a day's work, then back to the beach again. The farm was ninety minutes away at Waerenga-o-Kuri, which means something about the land of the mad dogs.'

'The days were so different then,' Winks recalls. 'The kids used to all have bikes and they'd just leave them everywhere and the next day go, "Oh, where did I leave my bike?" And it'd be out the front at someone's house.'

'Half the time they didn't worry about whose bike they got on,' Stu adds. 'If they were at Joe Bloggs's house at lunchtime, then Joe Bloggs fed them. If we had ten kids here, we fed them. At the end of the holiday, we went around and collected our bikes and our kids and went home.'

Stu remembers a photo of the old bach and there were 23 kids' bikes lined up along the fence.

'You can't do it now, though,' he says. 'It has definitely changed. The cars have got faster. There are some yahoos here now. It's not like it used to be.'

Stu uses the boats as a gauge, too.

'These days if you've got an eighteen-footer, you've got a small boat. And people go further out and there's more of them. We've been out here and counted the boat trailers and there could be eighty to a hundred boat trailers parked out here.'

Māhia used to have one tractor to launch the boats into the water. Now they have four. To buy a tractor key, you have to be part of the fishing club first.

'The fishing club is a couple of hundred bucks each year, and a tractor key is about a hundred bucks,' Stu says. 'It's cheap, really. You can't run your own tractor for that. You

ABOVE
Brett Wood and Simon
Gardiner are watched
by cows as they surf at a
remote beach break on
the peninsula.

OPPOSITE
A small wave breaks into
a remote bay near the
township.

It's always an adventure
surfing around Māhia.

A common dolphin
swims by for a look.

just go and grab the tractor and away you go.
We are in a prized position here because we
just watch and when there is a gap we hop
out. We've seen boats parked waiting to get
a tractor and they're round the corner out of
sight.'

Along with the fishing, waterskiing was
always a top priority for the Bridge family.
They all learnt to ski here.

'We'd come in and have dinner and then
we'd go out skiing till dark,' Stu remembers.
'Often, the sea would settle right down and
you'd have these glassy conditions. We'd have
four boats out there with a whole heap of kids
on the beach and all the mothers there and
we'd ski right until dark. These kids would ski
and ski and ski.'

They said the beach was perfect for kids.

'There wouldn't be too many places in
New Zealand with a beach as safe as that,' he
smiles. 'You never get swells in there, never.
It's unique, really. The other good thing about
Māhia is that you can always launch your boat.'

As a family, they also spent time collecting
shellfish — pipi at the estuary and tuatua
along the beach by the golf club. They'd make
pipi fritters.

Māhia had a special visitor in March 2007.
Moko was a female bottlenose dolphin who
loved to interact with people in the bay.

'One day, she just arrived,' Stu tells me.
'My friend Bill was on his boat and she started
to play with his crayfish pots, with the floats.
The next day, he went out there, the dolphin

arrived. So he went and got a ball and threw the ball. She used to play with it, and it went on from there. Every day, he'd go out and play with the dolphin.'

Winks and Stu were headed out fishing one day, but Moko was under their prop so they couldn't start the motor.

'There were some young kids there and we asked them to come over and get this dolphin away,' Winks recalls. 'So they came over and Moko followed them away.'

'And then she flogged their paddle — they couldn't paddle their canoe,' Stu adds. 'She would take the paddles off people all the time.'

Moko liked to take things, play with them and then bring them back. She would take them right up to the person she stole it off. As soon as they tried to grab it, she would flick it away again. She became quite annoying, and nearly drowned a woman one day by preventing her from swimming back to shore.

Moko also rescued a couple of whales in the bay once. The whales got caught in front of a sandbar that had formed.

'People were there trying to push these whales out,' Stu recalls. 'Next minute, Moko arrives. She collects the whale and the calf up and takes them around to the channel out to sea.'

Moko spent quite a few months in the bay before she made her way to Gisborne. There she went up the river and played for a while, before following a fishing boat to Whakatāne. They found her dead there not long after.

ABOVE
Andy Sutherland weighs
in a kingfish at 15 kilos.

OPPOSITE
Good, fighting kingies
on the edge of the
Continental Shelf, off
Māhia.

Many hands are needed
to fillet kingfish of this
size.

Andy collects a couple
of crays off Portland
Island.

—

When Melissa was 18 months old, Stu and Winks were told by doctors that she had a melanoma. It was removed shortly after, but her prognosis was not what any parent would ever want to hear.

'She had been in and out of hospital that many times,' Winks tells me. 'She was having bits removed but she didn't have any treatment — nothing like that.'

Stu remembers when Melissa played hockey and she'd had some skin grafts done on her leg. She had big balloons put in and couldn't run properly.

'She couldn't play hockey, so what does she do?' Stu asks. 'She went and refereed it. That just summed her up. That's just the way she did it. The way she looked at life all the way through.'

Poss lived her life at full speed as if she knew she had to make the most of it. She was like that right through our years at university. A real spark with a no-nonsense approach to enjoying our days there.

'University was a great part of her life,' Winks smiles. 'She loved it. She loved Palmerston North. She told me she was very, very happy and had great mates there.

'She had a great sense of humour. Her laugh was so loud. She loved fun. Everything was a big joke and she just got on with it. She did as much as she could.'

Derek Searancke first befriended Poss when she was in the hostel room across from him at Massey University in their first year. They instantly shared a strong bond. Martha Flynn was Poss's right-hand girl — equally as mischievous and the two were inseparable. They didn't surf often, but they weaved naturally into the surf crew.

'I remember her saying they loved going for adventures and walks along the beaches,' Winks says. 'She loved the trips to the Wairarapa and especially to White Rock. And she and Martha were tomboys.'

Poss developed her brain tumour while at Massey.

—

Last summer, almost 30 years since our first university adventure to Māhia, most of us reunited at Mokotahi for a few days. We were there to remember those hedonistic days of university, rekindle friendships and celebrate the life of our friend, Poss.

Māhia is one of the last great preserves of the New Zealand coastal lifestyle, where fisherman reign supreme and surfers thrive.

Bringing our children here feels like a revolution of the wheel, and if a little bit of Poss's infectious enthusiasm from her own time growing up here rubs off, then that's just fine.

Over those few days, Poss was omnipresent in our minds as we tapped back into the laughter and mateship that bound us all so tightly together, all those years ago. The stories flowed like wine. The nights shrank. The mornings started at first light like we didn't want to spill a drop.

—

The perfect sea state is exactly what Andy Sutherland was hoping for. Somewhere out on the horizon was the edge of the Continental Shelf. On his GPS, an X marked the location of a pinnacle that Andy spoke about with wide eyes full of promise.

Andy Sutherland lives in Wainui, with his wife De-Arne and their teenage girls Ella and Anika. Andy has an intense passion for fishing. He's determined to pass some of it on to the rest of us.

Nigel Bryce, Derek Searancke and Brett Wood are aboard and they're jostling for position, vying to be anointed as first mate —

hoping desperately that Andy might let them drive for a bit. I can't break it to them that I am second in charge. Self-elected, of course.

By the time we arrive at the pinnacle, the land is but a faint shadow on the horizon. We drop to 60 metres and Andy teaches us to jig. We're after kingfish and it's a physical game. Andy, then Derek, each land a 15-kilo torpedo that can barely fit into the chilly bin.

Brett gets the action wrong time and again, and he loses lure after lure because of it, much to our delight. He's lost around $120 worth of lures when it finally all comes together and he hooks a monster. The fight seems unfair, Brett against a beast from the depths. Eventually, he pulls the kingy in and it stretches the scales past 20 kilos.

I've never seen a fish like it — massive and beautiful at the same time.

Over the next few days, those kingfish, along with some crayfish we pick up diving, feed the entire group. We eat like kings as the chefs in our group come to the fore.

We sprawl around Mokotahi like some kind of Māhia royalty. Kids in swarms and adults engaging in deep, hearty lung laughs. I can imagine Poss looking down at us with her eyes as big as those of a possum. Loving every bit of banter, the evenings of laughter, reminiscences and chuckling at just how old we've all grown. She'd love that the place she introduced us to is the place we go back to, to spend quality time together.

THE ROBINSON CRUSOE DREAM

CLIVE NEESON — ŌAKURA,

TARANAKI

The entry to Clive Neeson's home
features large gates painted with a series of
waves and a surfboard strung into position
across the arch. It references aspects of Clive's
life: from carefree surf traveller to Indonesian
dreaming to filmmaking — this is the eclectic
lair of an adventure-seeking genius.

The front door leads to an open-plan
expanse that juts out into the Tasman Sea at
Ōakura like the stern of a ship about to set
sail. That's not by chance.

In his movie, *Last Paradise*, which took him
most of his life to make, Clive paints a picture
of surfers with childhood dreams of Robinson
Crusoe — living in a tree hut at a tropical
beach, with great surf out front.

'That was the model for designing this
place,' he says. 'I didn't have a tree big enough
to build a tree hut. So what I did was I built
a deck and planted the trees around it, and

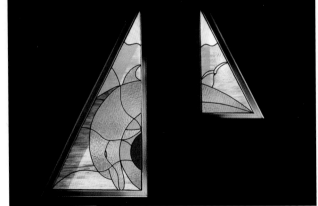

they grew into what looked like a tree hut. And that's the outlook from my lounge. When you look out my bay window, you look into the tree hut. And it feels like that Robinson Crusoe feeling every morning I wake up.'

As a child, Clive would fall asleep in his parents' campervan, or a tent, as his parents filmed wildlife throughout Eastern Africa during the 1950s.

'I feel more belonging than anywhere when I'm in my campervan, because that's where I received that security and love against the face of extreme danger in Africa with my parents,' he says. 'My time in Africa, when I was six years old, was some of the scariest but happiest times of my life.'

His family moved to Raglan not long after,

PREVIOUS SPREAD
Clive crosses farmland to access a favourite surf break along the Taranaki coastline.

TOP
Clive's Ōakura home draws reference from his travels to tropical locations.

OPPOSITE BELOW
The leadlight window that reminds him every day of the special place he lives.

ABOVE
The Robinson Crusoe-inspired tree-hut design.

Breakfast on the run.

where he learnt to surf and then cut his teeth as a young adult doing 'Silicon Valley-type work'. He was designing new, very high-tech electronics while studying physics and electronic engineering — building computers.

'I just didn't want to live in Silicon Valley,' he tells me. 'I was a surfer. I'd come from Raglan and I wanted to live in a place where I could have that every day, but still be able to work in the likes of Silicon Valley. Then I had this idea when I returned to New Zealand: why not build my own Silicon Valley at the beach?'

Taranaki immediately appealed to him. It had the beaches, waves and a great big snow-capped mountain. It also had an energy industry that he could develop technology for.

He found a piece of land, on the beach, that he could turn into a home and business base for his technology development.

'That's why the house is so big. Half of it became my little Silicon Valley on the beach. At three hundred square metres, it's a big house. It means you can, conceptually, go surfing whenever you want, but then work also, whenever you want. The design work was quite intense, but I found the surfs in between were really balancing.'

Clive would work six months in the northern hemisphere, and then six months based out of Ōakura. This was in 1984 — before the internet. He had a consulting relationship with STL, near Cambridge. Among many world-firsts, they invented fibre optics and pulse-code modulation, the foundation of the internet and the digital revolution. So they were able to design data communications with the northern hemisphere electronically.

'One of my first projects was for their robotic vision department, designing the circuitry to allow robots to "see",' he says. 'They were later able to use it as the world's first teleconferencing system, allowing UK surgeons to remotely supervise operations in Africa.

'In 1989, they asked me to create a 3D printing robot, which could build a prototype silicon chip directly from design plans. It took more than six months, so I designed and built it in their labs and finished programming

ABOVE
Clive in his happy place.

Some of the first
housings Clive made for
his cameras, more than
50 years ago.

OPPOSITE
From the top lounge,
Clive finds endless
inspiration — his creative
zone.

it remotely from Ōakura, using the very
same stuff that we had developed as the
communications device.'

In New Zealand's summer, Clive would
work for the energy industries, designing
customised computers for controlling
power stations and the first energy plants in
Taranaki and West Australia. At the same
time, he'd be doing the high-tech design in the
northern hemisphere.

'En route, there was always a stopover,
somewhere like Bali or Mexico. When you're
going from the northern hemisphere to
the southern hemisphere, there's always a
tropical stopover that you can work into it.'

He admits that it boiled down to
maintaining his surf lifestyle.

'It was very early days for technology
development, but there was so much
innovation then and I wanted to be involved
in that, and pursue a career there, but still
not have to give up my surfing,' he reveals.
'I managed, in the end, to blend the two
together in this house.'

While he wanted his house to feature
a workspace, he never wanted an office
environment, opting instead to come and go
between his two lounges depending on which
felt the most conducive to work at the time.

'I don't like the idea of an office because
you're surrounded by these gadgets and décor
that look like work,' Clive smiles. 'My lounge
looks like the beach. That's a place where I'm
happy, so it makes me happy working there.'

Clive's surf travel took him through the
Pacific Islands, to Northwest Australia,
Indonesia and Eastern Africa. But it is Ōakura
that stole his heart.

'Ōakura has a microclimate,' he explains.
'It's north-facing, and it's sheltered from the
cold southerly winds by the ranges on the
mountain behind it. In winter, the sun passes

ABOVE
Not a bad backyard for
a surf- and kitesurf-
obsessed 65-year-old.

OPPOSITE
Kite surfing has given
Clive a new appreciation
for his coastline.

low and reflects off the sea and it illuminates the inside of the house. It provides this beautiful central heating that most other places don't get. The north-facing aspect creates this settled ocean where the waves wrap in much cleaner, just like they do at Whale Bay and Ahipara.'

He says Taranaki is perfect for surfing half the time and perfect for kitesurfing the other half. He reckons six days out of seven, he's engaged in one or the other.

Clive's 65 and shows no sign of slowing down. He reminds me of a teenager as he watches the ocean and gets excited by a wind shift. We watch the waves from the crow's-nest upper storey of his house and I can see him debating between kitesurfing and surfing.

'Taranaki is a world-class destination for kitesurfing,' he says. 'But it's rocky; the winds can be extreme and the waves can be big. Most kiteboarders want onshore winds and ride a wakeboard-type thing. We ride a surfboard and we ride the waves just like a surfer. Cross-shore to cross-off is what we prefer, for the perfection of the wave and to be able to best tap the wind power.'

He looks at me as if analysing my ability to grasp the next concept he is about to deliver.

'The great thing about Taranaki is the strongest wind is always at the Venturi point — where the wind increases because it's squeezing around an obstacle, which is the mountain,' he explains. 'Because it's a curved coastline with a conical mountain, it always has a Venturi spot at one particular place around the coast — on any particular day and on any wind direction. So we're able to pick a windy spot, almost every day, where the direction is perfect cross-shore. And on the same day, we can drive around the coast a bit more and then find an offshore spot that we can surf. There are only a handful of guys that kitesurf the point breaks here. We have it all to ourselves, like we used to in the early days with surfing.'

The additional benefit, he tells me, is that you can get about 35 waves in a session without needing to paddle. It's like tow-in surfing, using the natural forces of the wind instead of a jet ski.

Clive doesn't like the term 'retirement', preferring instead to invest his energy into giving back with involvement in community projects.

'Nothing I do these days is financially remunerative,' he says. 'From about the age of fifty, my work didn't involve earning money. It involved community projects and creative projects, such as film. I switched. So I didn't retire, I'm just as busy now as I've ever been. But it's about creating community and a good lifestyle.'

The turning point coincided with making *Last Paradise*, which involved a lot of money — albeit all flowing in the wrong direction.

'But that was fine — the high-tech business, physics, electronic, engineering, was extremely remunerative,' he says. 'Developing control systems for power stations and gas platforms — that was combining the two highest-paying industries: electronic technology and energy.'

I wonder how many people saw him out surfing and thought, *There's that bum over there. He's never going to do any good in life; he's out surfing again today.*

'Any surfers who saw me, they just understood,' Clive says. 'I believe in finding what you really want to do in life early and believing in it. Then shaping your life to accommodate that dream. And don't get caught up in other people's dreams.

'Just have a great dream when you're a kid. If you have a great dream when you're a kid about what life should be, it probably won't change. The rest of your life should be manifesting that in the best way you can.'

—

Over breakfast early the next morning, Clive tells me a story from when he was working in the UK and visited a castle. In the distance, across the fields, was a miniature Arc de Triomphe — it could have come straight out of Paris. He asked the guard, 'What's that thing there for?' And the guard replied, 'That was for the king to be able to have a view — something to look at from that window. It's called a folly.'

'When I came back and bought this place, it was just a shack. I looked down the coastline and it was all wasteland and boxthorn and scrub, no trees,' he recalls.

'And that was my whole view. And I thought, *Well, I could never afford to build a folly, an Arc de Triomphe, but I like the concept.* What I could afford was to buy a tree for five dollars, or maybe a thousand trees for five dollars, and nature would build the rest in thirty years' time. And then we could make a pathway through it that we could cycle through to the surf breaks — a tree tunnel suitable for all weather.'

A few surfing mates shared the idea, so they joined forces. The first tree went into the ground in 1985, and now, when he looks out his favourite window, Clive sees a tree-lined coast with beautiful pōhutukawa flowering each Christmas.

'We dreamed it and nature built it,' he smiles. 'But we provided nature with the seed. I love that every day I get to see it on the coast — to cycle down it and to be able to go surfing.'

Last light as Clive finds a
running wave at Ōakura.

Clive had two dreams in life: to create a film and a nature trail, both with the goal to get people out into the outdoors, loving nature and recreating. The 3-kilometre walkway is a community project and accesses three surf breaks that he often kitesurfs as well.

'It also creates part of a larger cycleway, which is twenty kilometres,' he adds. 'It provides an access to a loop of beautiful country roads.'

Clive hopes one day to see all of Taranaki's famous surf breaks accessible by bicycle, to eliminate the 'Taranaki shuffle' — the practice of driving up the road in your car to check a spot, coming back down the next road, and so on.

'My aim for this community is to provide a network of walkways, where people don't need to use cars,' Clive explains. 'They could use bikes and scooters and travel through tree tunnels and nature walkways. So kids can walk to school, people can ride their bikes to the surf breaks. And in Taranaki, these need to be sheltered walkways, because of the wind and the harsh weather. It has multiple benefits for the community; it combats depression, obesity, climate change, traffic congestion and brings back the birdsong, which increases with every year.'

He says Taranaki is a conversion spot for many people he met around New Zealand. They all had the same idea, shared the same dream in life. They came together here and formed a community of outdoor recreators.

'We have so much in common. We have a cohesion here, which is based around adventure sports. And that's a wonderful thing because there's excitement during the day and there's a common love of nature.'

It was right out in front of his house where Clive had one of those magical moments in the Tasman Sea.

'During the first year I was here, I went for a bodysurf out the front. The sun was just rising and I bodysurfed this wave when a dolphin jumped right beside me, right out in front of the wave. Behind it was the green foothills and the snowy mountain. That experience was indelibly imprinted on my mind. So when I built this house, I designed a leadlight window for my bedroom, so that when the sun rose every morning, it would illuminate my room with that vision again, for the rest of my life. That was the first wonderful experience and there have been thousands since.'

Before Covid, Clive usually skipped town for the five harshest months of winter. He'd go somewhere tropical, like Mauritius, Zanzibar, Indonesia, the Pacific Islands or Mexico. Then in spring he'd return via Northwest Australia, where he'd split his time between surfing up in the desert and his house in Perth.

'It's sunshine all the way,' he laughs. 'Camping along the Ningaloo Coast where it's kitesurfing and surfing, every day.'

He's been visiting the area for the past 25 years.

ABOVE
Clive is as happy falling
asleep in his campervan
as he is anywhere.

OPPOSITE
(Clockwise from left)
Riding to the surf breaks
near his home, through
a tunnel of pōhutukawa,
has ticked off one of
Clive's life goals.

The Robinson Crusoe
dream has steered
Clive's way of life.

Ōakura is a sandy gem
in a rocky Taranaki
coastline.

'It's a really creative place in the desert; a very spiritual place and it has the best combination of surfing and kitesurfing in the world. And the wildlife in the ocean is amazing. It's the most preserved piece of coastline left in the world. That was the conclusion of the movie. The very place that was so ugly and no one wanted to go there, that was the one that survived.'

People from all nationalities find themselves attracted to Clive, and he often becomes a sounding board for people to express their issues to.

'It gives me a great insight. When you're working alongside them, you're out travelling with them and you get to hear their stories from their point of view. And they confide in you. I don't know if it's being a Kiwi that does that, but they tell me that they don't do that to everyone.'

Clive said his upbringing in Eastern Africa had something to do with it. He grew up in a country where everyone was African or Indian except him and his brothers.

'We weren't in South Africa. In East Africa, the Africans dominated and you fitted in. When we weren't home-schooling on safari, I was the only white fellow in my class at school. I learnt their language and tried to be part of their world. People in New Zealand think you're from South Africa all the time, and often they didn't even know that the Swahili world and Tanganyika even existed. But East Africa was and still is a really cool

place. What Kiwis often don't know is that there was a big slice of Africa, way bigger than South Africa, where the white people had a great relationship with the black people. They were always laughing together and they had a symbiosis that was really neat.'

He admits he leads a semi-nomadic life, but feels he understands more than most what home means. His mother was an orphan — with 'no parents, no childhood, no home'. She was gutsy and made it to Africa on her own.

'I was raised in a way that the whole world was my home. I could make a home anywhere. A lot of my youth was spent in a campervan in Africa, travelling between remote nursing stations. The wilderness was teeming with wild animals then — always with a sense of danger. When I was a kid, the sense of danger was a lion prowling around the tent or the campervan. When I'm in the desert in Western Australia, it's the adrenaline from the waves. But the feeling is the same — falling asleep in the campervan, just the serenity of that simple act.

'That's what home is to me.'

RIGHT
A sunset session down the beach from Clive's home.

OPPOSITE
One more wave on dark . . .

THE ADVENTURERS OF TATA BAY

LISA SAVAGE AND TONY BATEUP

— TATA BEACH, GOLDEN BAY

At the northern end of the Abel Tasman National Park, Tata Bay sparkles. It's one of the best-kept secrets in the dazzling array of beaches and inlets that the area has become famous for. Only the most adventurous discover its stunning coastline — complete with two of the most ecologically important islands in the entire park.

It's fitting that respected adventurers and former multi-sport athletes Tony Bateup and Lisa Savage should call this home. It's also where they work — teaching people to paddle and imparting their love for adventure and exploration out on the sea that laps at their path.

Tony and Lisa bought Golden Bay Kayaks at Tata Beach in February 2010. They had been involved in farming for quite a while, including owning a dairy farm in Matariki, Tapawera. Their son, Kye, was born around that time also. Initially, they split their time between the two properties.

'For the first season, we were commuting between here and the farm,' Tony explains. 'We'd do the season down here, go up to Matariki for the winter, and then come back here for the summer. It made sense to base ourselves here year-round, which I'm pretty happy with, I have to admit.'

'If you squat there long enough, you end up owning it,' Lisa smiles.

—

From the deck, we gaze out across the back lawn. It's strewn with kayaks, paddles, life jackets, and has a small green booth that sells ice creams and adventure. A sandy path leads the 8 metres to the beach, and a lazy Tata Bay laps at the shore. The water is blue-green with distinctly tropical qualities.

Across the glassy surface, to the northwest, lie the Tata Islands: Ngawhiti and Motu.

'Tata means close,' Lisa says. 'Motu Island is actually connected by a sand bridge. On a king tide, you can walk almost all the way over to the island. It's knee-deep most of the way and then up to your waist at the end.'

Tony tells me that the islands are home to New Zealand's largest spotted shag colony.

'You've got the endangered reef herons out there — it is not unusual to see one of those,' he says. 'They are a beautiful bluey, smoky grey colour all the way through. One of four heron species that breed in New Zealand.'

'You've also got New Zealand's best example of the milk tree, the tōwai or ewekuri, which is again endangered,' Lisa adds. 'They've been growing them in Wellington, in the Botanical Garden. When you cut the trees, it looks like milk, hence the name. Then we've got the whārangi —

PREVIOUS SPREAD
Lisa, Tony and Kye paddle around Ngawhiti Island, part of the Tata Islands, which they can see from their home on Tata Beach.

ABOVE
Fresh herbs from the garden.

Dinner with the family in the lead-up to Christmas.

OPPOSITE
Wainui Falls is a favourite spot to visit for Lisa, Tony and Kye.

a native lemon tree. This is the most southern point that it'll grow. We've got the New Zealand passionfruit on Motu Island. The islands are ecologically the most important islands in the Abel Tasman.'

Tony and Lisa don't just have a passing interest in the flora and fauna in their backyard. When they first arrived, they ran the trapping programme on the islands. They are also active in little blue penguin conservation.

'We took over the trapping programme when we bought the business,' Tony tells me. 'It's not part of what we needed to do, but it is just part of who we are. Peter Geen, one of the local artists, has come on board and he's driving that now.'

Lisa tells me that they caught 12 stoats in the first two years.

'We were running the trap lines catching rats, stoats, rats, stoats, or rat, rat, rat,' Tony adds. 'They were swimming across from the mainland.'

Lisa says stoats can swim up to 2.5 kilometres.

'The rats were just phenomenal, we were killing rats the whole time,' Tony says. 'And then you slowly get on top of that. And once their numbers start coming down, you start catching stoats. They are a bit of a glory one to catch. They are smart. They'll sit and look at a trap and run around it and then carry on. They don't need to go in there for any good reason.'

ABOVE
The Golden Bay Kayaks team prepares the boats for some customers.

OPPOSITE
Direct beach access from the boat shed.

Something for everyone.

A group prepares for adventure.

Even with more than 10 years watching this view, Tony describes it as 'absolutely phenomenal'.

'I love the changing tides,' he tells me. 'I go out there at high tide and think, *This is my favourite*. And then I go out there at low tide and think, *No, this is definitely my favourite time*. It's always changing and evolving. And we get lots of wildlife — lots of seals and stingrays and dolphins.'

Lisa says the dolphins aren't always here at the height of summer, and she wonders if they go and feed off the Taranaki Bite.

They have a resident pod of Hector's dolphins that visit regularly most of the year. It is noted when they occasionally disappear for a period of time. The wildlife changes with the seasons, and with each year.

'I feel like we see more orca than common dolphins,' Tony says. 'We're here more often now, but it seems to me that orca are coming through more regularly. In the past five years, I think we've paddled with them more than ever. Kye's paddled with them three or four times and he's at school most of the time. They've hung around for a good couple of hours each time as well. When the dolphins are here, they seem to be on the move. They are on a mission and not hanging out with us.'

The novelty of living in a place like this hasn't worn off for Tony or Lisa. They still get a buzz every time they head out — in both strong winds and in completely calm conditions.

'Kye and I went out a couple of weeks ago and had a great time together,' Tony says. 'Kye is a really smart kid — everything is calculated. He'll just wait until he's ready to do it. We got the surf skis out and he's like, "Oh, nah. I don't really want to go." It was probably blowing fifteen to twenty knots. We went out there and he surfed some waves and his eyes grew big. Seeing him getting some enjoyment out of what we're doing is incredible. This doesn't have to be the sport that he chooses, but I would like to see him become proficient in a kayak, understand the ocean and have some knowledge of it. It was one of those moments for me that it was like, *Man, this is probably one of the coolest paddles I've had in a long, long, long time* — just sharing that with Kye.'

Kye, 11, is a top mountain biker for his age. He has the genes — both his parents were élite athletes when mountain biking was first emerging. He's in a good place for it — the trails around Golden Bay, across the Takaka Hill and in Nelson are world-class.

Tony grew up in Karamea on the West Coast. When he was nine, his family moved to Nelson. He spent most of his life there until he made the move over to Golden Bay in 2007.

In his youth, he took up motocross racing until he saw one of the first mountain bikes in a local shop.

'I got one and thought, *Far out, this is amazing,*' he recalls. 'I stopped doing motocross and started doing more mountain biking. I found it heaps more social and easier to get out and about with other people.'

He's quite coy about his achievements, but he won a couple of Junior Downhill Mountain Biking Championships in New Zealand and was invited to a special Mount Fyffe downhill race. Organisers ferried riders to the top of the Kaikōura peak with helicopters — it was a landmark race at the time.

In the early 1990s, his ambition led him to adventure racing and multi-sport.

'It was actually Nathan Fa'avae who got me into kayaking,' Tony recalls. 'He was going through NMIT and was looking for people to train for kayaking. He said he would teach me how to paddle, so away we went.'

ABOVE
There aren't many
places in the world
where you can paddle
to your own deserted
beach.

OPPOSITE
Tony and Lisa know this
coastline intimately.

There's adventure every
day as the family explore
the islands.

The family dog, Mac,
swims for shore while
Kye takes his mates for
a paddle in front of their
house.

He said that, like most Kiwis, he just plodded away at it, gained a few skills, and when the passion took hold he started to work harder.

'It becomes fun and you're doing it a bit more often,' he adds. 'Then everything started leading towards the adventure-racing path.'

His highlight in terms of results came as a team result in 2005 when the World Championships were held in Westport. They finished fourth.

'We were motivated,' remembers Lisa, who was part of the team. 'Because Nathan said that Sāmoa had a better chance of winning a Rugby World Cup than what Port Nelson had of finishing in the top ten.'

Tony believes the results were never that

important to him. He raced for fun and to challenge himself.

'The single-biggest thing I learnt through that time was that you can go a lot longer, harder, further, faster than I would have ever thought,' he smiles. 'You are almost superhuman. You can go days without sleep — you're quite phenomenal.'

They both admitted that competing together sometimes grated on their relationship.

'I was a bit rough on Lisa sometimes, maybe,' he says. 'Sometimes, because I knew what Lisa was capable of, and if it's not quite there, it's like, "Come on, you can do better than this."'

'Tony used to get pissed off because I didn't

train like he did,' she laughs.

'She'd take the cows for a walk in the morning and that would be her training for the day. It's like, "Oh, no, that will be good enough."'

'And it was,' Lisa says.

Lisa is a fourth-generation Golden Bay girl, making Kye fifth-generation.

'My great-grandfather planted the pine trees at Farewell Spit,' she tells me. 'We are very slow breeders on the Harwood side. My great-great-grandfather is James Harwood — as in the Dunedin Harwood, the little township down there. He was made famous by refusing to drench his sheep in the 1840s. It was a government edict and he refused to do so. There is a lot of his equipment in the museum in Dunedin — he was also a doctor. James is his son, who then came up to work on the lighthouse and then they moved to Upper Tākaka. There they started up the pub, which was known as The Rat Trap — it was quite infamous in New Zealand. It was under the licence of my grandad but it was Aunt Sylvie who ran it, because women couldn't hold licences for public places.'

The Rat Trap was burned down in a domestic incident on 19 May 1994.

—

Lisa's parents bought the Tata Beach bach in 1984 to give them some respite from the summer winds that would blow for weeks on

Lisa paddles into a cave along the coastline.

end up the valley. There was a wetland at the back, and the original boat shed was built by the Christophers, who had bought the land.

Lisa can remember always being very competitive.

'I was at a five-year-old birthday party and had to win every single game,' she remembers. 'I didn't give a shit. I just wanted to win every single one.'

Lisa started playing netball when she was 13, and it wasn't until she returned from her OE in 1998 that she started racing mountain bikes.

Her small size and fighting spirit fitted well with mountain biking. Lisa represented New Zealand at the World Mountain Biking Championships and competed internationally. She was quickly picked up by the well-respected Diamondback Racing Team. Lisa narrowly missed selection for the Commonwealth Games one year.

Since Kye arrived, Lisa and Tony have scaled right back on competing, apart from a few memorial and specialty events that they do for fun.

'Your priorities shift with kids coming along,' Lisa says. 'I think that's really important because you see all these old multi-sporters who hang on to the past and they continue their career with their kids. The kids get dragged up waiting for their parents.'

'Once you've got kids, it's not your turn anymore — it's their turn,' Tony adds. 'You can do one thing really, really, really well. You can do two things pretty good, but you can't do three things well. So you can't have a family, work and a sport. It just doesn't work.'

That life is still important to Tony and he follows the results.

'It was pretty cool that we got a chance to compete in the glory days of adventure racing and multi-sport in New Zealand. It was fun —

you did it because it was fun and not because you were results-driven.'

They've been able to apply some of the things they learnt through sport to running the business.

'Our sport has taught us quite a high level of tenacity,' Lisa says. 'It teaches you tolerance and intolerance. You've got a level of understanding, but then you've got a level of knowing, *Okay, at some stage that person does need to step up, because it's not that hard.*'

The northern end of Abel Tasman National Park gets a bad rap for its weather and sea-state extremes. It's misunderstood and often gets quickly shuffled into the 'too hard basket'.

'That's really frustrating,' Lisa says. 'With adventure racing, it's the same thing — actual versus perceived risk. Adventure racing is perceived as hardcore. Whereas actually it's just the perception that it's impossible, but you are your own limiter.'

She says the clientele has changed as well.

'Within the ten years we've had the business, we've gone from a population of independent paddlers to people needing everything done for them. Possibly that's the way Tourism New Zealand has portrayed our outdoor activities.'

Tony says a lot of people wanted to do an adventure without pushing themselves or having to do the work.

'Looking back over the years, our first customers wanted the best value for the day,' he says. 'They wanted the cheapest product for as long as they can get it. They would push hard and go a long way away and then come back again. They'd be having an amazing day. This is generalising, but a lot of our clients now are going out for half a day and not achieving very much distance and being exhausted at the end of it.

LEFT
Lisa, Tony and Kye
have an enviable
work–life balance.

OPPOSITE
The home business
means a constant
stream of people
are visiting the family,
which they love.

Kye looks to have
inherited some of his
parents' genes — he's a
top mountain-bike rider.

Lisa collects lemons
from the family orchard,
up the valley.

'We've changed our peripheral a wee bit as well,' he says. 'They probably did have a great day. We had to adjust our mindset — people don't need to go that far at all. And they are actually better at just staying within their limits. It's perfect for operations, because everyone is condensed.'

—

Golden Bay Kayaks has struggled through the Covid era. But Kiwis with a nose for adventure have still discovered them. That's been welcomed by Tony and Lisa, who take in young staff each year to help run the business.

'We've had a lot of kids come through here,' Lisa says. 'It's just part of what you do in rural areas and communities. People find a passion and they want to be involved. They perceive this as being an easy place to hang out, and a lot of them want to learn skills. I think as long as people are trying, or wanting to learn and they're fun to hang out with, then why not?'

Tony said they tried to take in workers who had gone through Tai Poutini Polytechnic or had done some sort of outdoor tourism course.

'If they're local kids, then we will generally give them a chance,' he tells me. 'What they learn in a season with us — if they were in a big corporate, it would take them five years to learn it. It's like doing an apprenticeship with a massive building company that only put doors on. Most of these guys are capable of running the business by the end of the season.'

Recently, Tony and Lisa started designing their own boats. John Dobbie was making the double sea kayaks and fibreglass versions of those over in Nelson, and he ended up getting fibreglass poisoning. He decided to sell the mould overseas so they couldn't be replicated here.

'My brother-in-law was keen to be involved in the project and to help design and build them — he is a composite designer at Dynamic Composites in Christchurch,' Tony says. 'We couldn't buy the fibreglass boat that we wanted, so we've come out with a better product — they have way more leg room than anything else on the market, they have way more storage and they handle really well. They have exceeded my expectations.'

They had planned to sell them, but by the time they finish each kayak season they're looking at what they are going to do for the off season. Whistler Bike Park has been the mainstay over recent years. Before Covid, they would try to spend seven to 10 weeks there each New Zealand winter.

—

Something about Tony and Lisa's story embodies all that is great about the New Zealand psyche and our quest for more, higher, further, better. They are living the quintessential Kiwi lifestyle without any caveats.

The morning that I'm leaving, Lisa and Kye accompany me, via Tākaka Primary School's new pump track.

Kye starts to lap around. I can see something fiery in his eyes. He finally clears a double that has been bothering him. That is when I realise that he has the genes from two incredible athletes and two inspiring people. The future may be a lot of things, but in Golden Bay it has a big heart.

ABOVE
With direct access to
the northern end of
Abel Tasman National
Park and the Tata
Islands, their Golden Bay
Kayaks business is a real
treasure.

THE DOCTORS' ESCAPE

We board the aptly named *Rosé* at Havelock Marina. The vessel is the gateway to another world — our destination is the Forrest family bach in Yncyca Bay, Pelorus Sound, Marlborough. We putt through the 8-knot zone before John eases forward on the throttle to get *Rosé* up on a plane. The noise of the engine washes across those onboard like a well-rehearsed cleansing ritual. The problems and stresses of the real world are left behind in the white wake that bubbles behind us.

Dr John Forrest and Dr Brigid Forrest founded and run Forrest Estate Wines. They describe it as 'a large boutique winery', which exports 70 per cent of its production. During John's tenure in the industry, he has been involved in some New Zealand firsts: the establishment of New Zealand Winegrowers; the New Zealand screw-cap initiative; Appellation Marlborough Wine;

and the most recent innovations to master the production of low-alcohol wine, something that has reinforced New Zealand's reverence on the global wine map. John's passion and involvement was recognised by his peers in 2019 when he was awarded a Lifetime Achievement Award by Wine Marlborough, and in 2020 when he was made a Fellow of New Zealand Winegrowers.

John and Brigid are accompanied on this journey by their daughter, Beth, 35, and her partner, Blair, with his two girls, Poppy, 13, and Charli, 11. Beth's older brother, Reid, 38, is sailing back from the Tasman Sea after completing marine-monitoring work in the Taranaki Basin. He's hoping to meet us the next day. Their younger brother, Sam, 30,

lives in Auckland. I join John at the helm in the cabin where he steers *Rosé* effortlessly, referencing the strands of past excursions on his GPS navigation screen.

Over the engine's rumble, he tells me the only criterion to build in the Marlborough Sounds is that you should be on the south side facing north — so that you get the maximum sun in winter.

'Our site filled that criteria, but at first we didn't like it when we were looking at it from the water. But when you get up there and turn around, it is just fantastic,' he grins. 'I bought it with my brother for $37,000 in 1991. We knew it was a bargain for 100 acres and nearly a kilometre of beachfront.'

The brothers were planning to sit on it, but

PREVIOUS SPREAD
The Forrest family run out onto their jetty for a swim in Yncyca Bay.

ABOVE
The bach is tucked into native bush.

OPPOSITE
Jumping off the jetty is one of many family traditions.

Unloading gear from *Rosé*.

John and Brigid, with their daughter Beth and her partner Blair, and his children Poppy, 13, and Charli, 11.

their mother had other ideas.

'My mother said, "No, I've wanted all my life to have a place in the Sounds, and now you boys are back from around the world we're going to do it."'

They prefabricated the house in a shed in Renwick and put it on a barge. They had to use a digger as a crane to carry the pieces up across the foreshore and back to the site — just small loads all day because of the mud. It took three weeks to assemble. By 1992, the family had a bach in Yncyca Bay.

'Other than putting a railing on the deck once the grandchildren started to come, it hasn't changed,' John tells me. 'We wanted a bach, not a fancy house. I wanted glass everywhere and Bob O'Malley, the builder, said, "No, no, no. I know how strong the winds are down here and you're not having all that glass."'

Bob built the house to well beyond the required building standards to further strengthen the bach for the high winds that can occur here. During their first long weekend stay, John was pleased Bob had.

'We were here for three or four days,' John remembers. 'We had a massive southerly storm with williwaws coming in and slamming into the windows — you could watch the windows flexing. I didn't sleep because I was worried about the boat on the mooring. And then the weather swung straight around to a northwesterly storm. The house got slammed from two directions, but it stood like a rock. I knew Bob's advice was right. It was frightening.'

John was mostly raised by his mother and she loved the Sounds. She'd spend weeks at the bach with her younger brother and his wife and her beloved sons, daughters-in-law and grandchildren.

'The only good thing about losing my father

when I was eight is that I had an incredibly
competent mother who was a superwoman,'
he says. 'This is going back into the '60s
now. I went to university and I was looking
strangely at women who were ripping their
bra off and burning them. I thought, *What
are you on about? Here you are at university. You
are smarter probably most of the time than I am,
and more capable.* I had come from having
a superwoman as a mother who could do
anything. I suppose I'd been through women's
liberation already.

'My mum loved this place. Her ashes are
here,' John tells me. 'One weekend, we all
came down — the three brothers and all the
family — and we had a wonderful weekend
here. And as the last afternoon came to an
end, the youngest grandchild said, "When are
we going to throw Grandma away?" No one
wanted to finally do it.'

John said she was the reason they didn't
have a TV in the bach.

'Grandma wouldn't allow it, and since
she's died no one's really wanted it,' he adds.

Beth and her brothers would use their time
at the bach to train for sports events, running
the tracks and up to the top of the mountain
and swimming around the mussel rafts.

'There would be a lot of rowdy games,
card games and particularly competitive
Monopoly,' she laughs.

Brigid's mother taught her grandkids
to play Mahjong when they were about
10. It only ever gets played at the bach.
Trivial Pursuit is always hotly contested,
although Beth believes the 1970s version
is skewed in John and Brigid's favour. Then
there were rainy afternoons of Scrabble and
Bananagrams.

'When we were kids, Uncle Peter, who's
the accountant, used to send us all bankrupt
in two-day-long games of Monopoly,' Beth

ABOVE
It's difficult to keep the kids of all ages out of the water.

OPPOSITE
Abandoning ship after tying *Rosé* to a mooring.

Swimming in the bay is a favourite pastime for Brigid.

The resident stingray inspects the jetty.

recalls. 'Monopoly used to get quite vicious, and Peter wasn't happy until everybody was bankrupt and he was the winner. He was always the banker.'

We arrive at the wharf in Yncyca Bay and decant the bags and boxes of wine to the dwelling. Brigid drives a 4WD 'Mule' to speed up the process. John's first thoughts are to dinner. He, Blair and Beth soon scout out enough seafood and we all relax back on the deck enjoying the view.

Over mussels cooked to perfection, accompanied by carefully matched Forrest wines, Brigid tells me that their bach in Yncyca Bay is an essential bolthole for the family.

'People will always tell you that for every one night in the Sounds, you feel like you've been away for three or four — you just settle into the rhythm of the land and the seasons. You don't have to do anything, or you can go hiking up to the top of the mountain, or go fishing for the day, go exploring, or just sit on the deck or beside the fire and do nothing.'

Brigid says their kids have a real attachment to this place.

'Our youngest held the record for number of guests,' she smiles. 'We had six girls and six boys here for seven days when they were about sixteen. They were crammed in here with John and me for New Year's. Four of them managed to swim across from Fairy Bay to here.'

Reid is happiest when he's on the water, Brigid tells me.

'Whether he's on top of it or underneath it — that's his life. He's a marine scientist, and it is his leisure. His ideal would be to live somewhere like this, away from people. As children, they knew that it was fine to opt out and just have time to themselves — to read, play games, do mindless stuff.'

In 2006, the bay got power for the first time, but it didn't change the culture that much.

'You just didn't have to light the fire for everything, that's all,' John says. 'The gas fridge was small when we didn't have power, so you could put more beer and wine in once we got power.'

—

Brigid grew up in Taranaki and used to do a lot of swimming in the surf and bodysurfing. She met John on their first day at medical school at the University of Otago.

'She made me work unreasonably hard,' John laughs.

He tells me Brigid was talented and got into medical school first time around, while he went into neurophysiology. After four years, they finally said John could go into medical school, but he said 'no thanks'. He had other things to do. He went and did a PhD in neurophysiology.

They spent 10 years in Dunedin, before spending two years in San Diego, where they had their first child, Reid, and almost four years in Adelaide, which is where Beth was born.

Brigid had just bought into a promising general practice in Adelaide when John had 'an incredible desire' to bring his knowledge back to New Zealand and establish these new technologies in scientific research.

After 18 months in Palmerston North, John became disillusioned with the future of Kiwi research sciences, so they pursued an opportunity in the wine industry, buying land initially in Hawke's Bay, hoping to meld his day job with weekend grape-growing. However, John then reconnected with a new and exciting Marlborough — so different from what he had left as an 18-year-old — and moved back home to Marlborough, his family and his history.

'The Marlborough wine industry was just starting in 1988,' John recalls. 'We had collected and drunk wine in California where we lived and worked, and then in South Australia. So we had an appreciation and a love of wine. I started drinking wine seriously as a senior student at Otago University. It all coalesced. People thought we were taking a big risk, but we didn't even consider failing. We packed up the Ford Falcon and headed off to a tin garage that sat on mainly bare land with a small apple orchard in Renwick, Marlborough.'

From their 70 hectares of bare land, they developed seven vineyards.

'The loose plan was to make 2000 cases and sell it during the summer months from the cellar door; make a nice little living and then spend ten months of the year living the good life, really, and looking after the kids,' John says. 'Brigid was back full-time in medicine. In 1988, the New Zealand wine industry was at a million dollars export . . . now, it's two billion. We've followed that same trend.'

These days, Forrest Estate Wines is doing 100,000 cases and they expect to double that over the next two years — if they can get the grapes. Most of that demand is driven by their ability to make high-quality, natural, low-alcohol wine, a technique they pioneered.

Reid Forrest brings up a whopper crayfish from a crack in the reef they call The Refrigerator.

'It was never planned,' John tells me. 'It wasn't a dream. It just evolved and we've rolled along with our success.'

The whole way through the growth of the wine business, Brigid worked in medicine. Firstly, as a GP obstetrician.

'At one stage there, when we were rapidly developing the vineyard and the winery and having our third child, she was doing over 100 deliveries a year,' John laughs. 'Half the local kids go, "That's the doctor who delivered me."'

Brigid then retrained. She became a community geriatrician, working between general practice, the patients' homes and the local hospital. More recently, she retrained in palliative care, and she's now a doctor at the Marlborough Hospice. Brigid has also been on the Nelson Marlborough District Health Board for the past six years.

'She's our saint,' Beth smiles. 'When she was a practising GP, she was still the GM of finances, HR and everything else for Forrest Wines, while being mum to three kids.'

I suggest cheekily to John that that must make Brigid the brains of the wine operation.

'Yes, depending on how you define the brain,' he responds. 'In terms of the organisational structure — the i-dotting and t-crossing — then definitely. If you're talking about the creative side of winemaking, well, I have more ideas every day than most people have in a year, that's just the nature — I'm creative. Admittedly, a lot of those ideas are stupid. Beth's job, in her role now, is to harness the good ones and quietly deflect and discard the others.'

Beth, who has moved into the general manager role for the family business in recent years, describes herself as Captain Steady.

'Working with your family is the best thing and the worst thing you'll ever do,' she says. 'At the end of the day, Dad and Mum are amazing — going into a second generation, it's most important that you take time to stop, sit down and talk over a beer. So that is what we try to stick to.'

Beth has a team of 24 that includes 17 full-timers. She said her mother was a fount of knowledge when it came to managing people.

'One of my staff told me recently that they appreciate how we didn't dwell on mistakes,' Beth explains. 'That's something my parents taught me: it's not worth laying blame on anything. Don't sweat the small stuff. Fix it and get on with it.'

Unfortunately for Reid, the family business didn't quite work for him. He has an allergy to alcohol.

'It runs in my side of the family,' Brigid says. 'Unfortunately, some Irish lack a particular enzyme. I've got two nieces who are totally intolerant of alcohol, too. Even if we put alcohol in the Christmas pudding, unless it is well and truly flamed off, he will feel instantly nauseated and have headaches. He tried hard to appreciate what we did as a family when he was a teenager . . . with dire consequences on those first occasions. Having said that, he still likes the smell of it, and he has quite a good nose.'

Reid's dream was to spend his life working as a marine scientist, in an environment that he loves and which is also his hunting ground.

'Reid must have been eighteen and we had friends staying down here at the bach,' Brigid

tells me. 'Reid and Sam had been fishing off the wharf and observing this group of kingfish coming past, circling the bay about every two hours on calm mornings. We were all sitting up here eating breakfast and then there was a shout from Reid who had jumped in the water with his speargun.'

Reid had shot a 25-kilogram kingfish with a tiny speargun.

'There's not much of him now, and there was even less then,' Brigid laughs. 'It was dragging him around the bay. He was shouting at Sam, "Load the other spear! Load the other spear and bring it out to me!"'

'Sam had to strip off his clothes, load the spear and swim out about fifty metres to Reid,' John recalls. 'This is about half an hour into the fight by now. We were all down there watching. He got a headshot with the second spear and that slowed it down. He dragged it to the beach and I remember he was holding the fish up, ecstatically happy.'

Brigid tells me he got it up to the bach and then literally collapsed with exhaustion.

—

The next morning, we wake early for a fishing trip. Reid hasn't slept or eaten since arriving back late in the evening from the Taranaki Basin, but he's determined to join us, launching with his own boat and meeting us in the Sounds.

Over toast, we gaze across to the far side of the sound where the sun is illuminating regenerating native bush in the hills above Fairy Bay and North West Bay. I can't help but think there is an irony in the name Forrest — John's great-grandfather was among those who felled large tracts of native timber from the Marlborough Sounds in those early days, including the ridge across the water.

OPPOSITE
(Clockwise from left)
Reid returns from The Refrigerator with dinner.

Beth lands a stunning kingfish.

Yep, that's a 57-centimetre crayfish.

A chilly bin full of the best food available in Pelorus Sound.

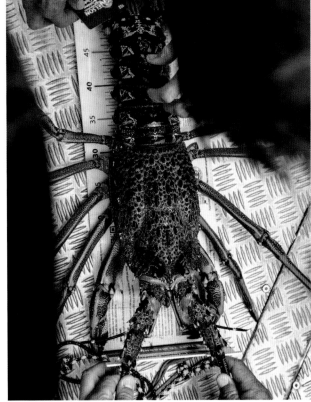

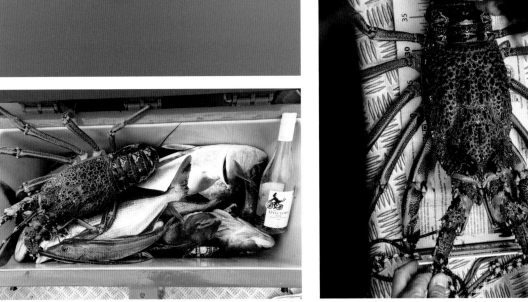

'They were the bosses for the Brownlee's Milling Company. Imagine stripping all the bloody trees back.' John shakes his head.

'John feels very guilty. That is why he plants trees,' Brigid tells me.

'Around the late 1860s, they started in Southland and then came up here. They certainly did some bloody damage,' John says.

John is the fifth generation to live in Marlborough, and he feels a connection to the place. Planting trees is part of his plan to help reconcile the work of his forefathers.

'I want to put money into a tree fund so I can subsidise people planting native trees in Marlborough,' he says. 'I think something like that would be the sort of endowment that I'd like to set up.'

Up behind the Forrest family bach at Yncyca Bay, pine trees cloak the peaks.

'Our plan is probably to just let them fall over,' John smiles. 'We're going to let the natives compete and push them back. In the slightly wetter, more fertile gullies, I'd like to plant some kahikatea, which does well down here. My family milled a lot of kahikatea out of here, and lowland tōtara is fast-growing here as well. In terms of commercial woods, they would be the two best value, along with rimu. I'd like to specifically plant those three species in patches. In seventy years or a hundred years, you could sustainably mill some of it. I hope the rest of it would just grow back like everything you see over the other side of the sound there.'

ABOVE
John and Beth are both master chefs.

OPPOSITE
(Clockwise from left)
Fresh as you can get.
Reid fillets a kingy.

Reid Forrest.

Brigid Forrest.

John Forrest.

Mussels served with the perfect rosé.

Beth Forrest.

John and Brigid know the challenges. They once planted 250 pōhutukawa and southern rātā around their bach. Within two weeks, the possums had eaten every single one of them.

'Evidently, baby pōhutukawa are a delicacy for possums,' Brigid smiles.

—

After some initial trouble with the motor on his new boat, Reid makes his way to the wharf and joins us for our fishing adventure. John dials up Spot-X on the chart plotter and we speed down Pelorus Sound. We're first targeting blue cod, then kingfish, then we'll drop Reid into The Refrigerator — a cave that lies in four to five metres of water at low tide and extends more than two body-lengths under a rock shelf — to dive for some crays. Reid goes straight to work preparing the fishing rods and lures.

Beth nudges her father and begs him to tell us about the story with her 90-year-old Uncle Doug.

'It was me, Uncle Doug, Reid and my nephew Bruce, who's a mobile butcher and a hunter-fisher,' John begins. 'The four of us came out fishing and we stayed the weekend. Reid and Bruce decided they would go hunt up the hill with the dogs and we could listen on the radios and keep an ear out for the dogs.

'Uncle Doug and I fished our way along the face in front of the bach, following the hunters up the hill. We were just along from the wharf here fishing and they were coming down the track. That's when the dogs got onto what was clearly a very large pig — we could see the bush moving as this pig came crashing down with the dogs in pursuit. The next moment, this pig appears — a big black Captain Cooker — on a cliff about twenty metres along from here, above the water.

'Luckily for the pig, it was high tide. The dogs come out of the bush and the pig just jumps into the water. Two of the dogs jump and follow him, and two of them stop. As soon as they get into the water, the dogs turn around and swim back to the beach. And this pig says, "I'm not going anywhere." So he struck out from the shore towards the other side of the sounds, but he made a fatal mistake. He swam straight towards our boat.

'Unbeknown to me, Uncle Doug had brought his World War Two Lee—Enfield .303. He casually wound the rod up and put it in the holder, walked into the cabin, and then I heard this *click, click*. I looked around and sure enough, Doug had the Lee—Enfield out the window. Well, that pig came right alongside the boat and foolishly selected the side where my pot-lifter was. Doug went *boom*. And the pig was stone dead.

'Before it sunk, I got the grappling hook, which had a rope attached under its arm, wrapped it around my pot-lifter, pressed the button and up it came. When Reid and Bruce finally made it down the hill, there was Doug quietly gutting this pig hung up on the side of the boat. You could see their eyes bulging out in disbelief. They didn't see the pig dive into the water.'

—

Sure enough, the first X on the map results in big fat blue cod — everyone reels one in. It feels more like we're walking around a market selecting produce as we go than fishing. At the next X, Beth hooks a giant kingfish and battles it to the surface. Each species that Reid lands is weighed, measured and photographed for Reid's Nelson Dawnbreakers Fishing Club contest. He tells me he's currently at the top of the table for the season so far. All he needs

now is a couple of crayfish and maybe a moki to shore up his position.

He finds those at The Refrigerator. Reid is a man of few words. From the surface, I watch him calm himself before gliding towards the bottom and disappearing into the murkiness. A minute later, he emerges with a large crayfish lassoed to his rope. When we get it to the surface, I realise it is the biggest one I have ever seen — 57 centimetres from its front claws to its tail.

It's a successful day's fishing by all accounts. We're back at the bach before lunch.

John quickly opens some wine to match our haul, then he and Beth go to work in the kitchen, as if they're in a *MasterChef* cook-off. John presents us with some delicious battered blue cod bites. Beth places a bowl of kingfish ceviche on the table. It melts in your mouth with a fresh tanginess that is exquisite.

We laugh and joke about the morning's events as we watch over our kingdom below, sipping a tasty low-alcohol rosé. I can see why Yncyca Bay has weaved its magic into the Forrests' hearts.

PREVIOUS SPREAD
The bach is positioned
perfectly for all-day sun.

RIGHT
Dusk over Pelorus
Sound from the deck of
the Forrest family bach.

SINCLAIR'S BACH

PETER AND LYNNE LAURENCE —

14 MILE, WEST COAST

Some baches seem impossible. Sinclair's Bach is one of them. It sits atop a stack of volcanic rock that has fingers reaching for 100 metres into the Tasman Sea. It has the presence of a ship that has run aground on the rocks with the precision of a surgeon and the optimism of an artist.

For more than 100 years, it has captivated the many who have called it home for a night or, for the lucky few, for longer. Its origins lie somewhere between the hut for a gold claim on the beach to some brave, inspired soul with a fascination for the elements of the West Coast. Probably both — history points to a woman who loved the coast and was also a miner.

One thing is certain. A night in the bach at 14 Mile, along the road between Greymouth and Westport, is a night with the Tasman Sea singing lullabies and the haunting

echoes of the rolling rocks below.

When Peter Laurence returned to New Zealand from France after his father died, he couldn't find anything he could afford, or liked, in Christchurch. He and Lynne had been coming to the West Coast for 'naughty weekends', and so he decided to look for a bach on the coast.

'Everybody said, "Go to Sinclair's Bach,"' he recalls. 'I came up here and I saw the place. The owner, Bruce Sinclair, was hoping to be able to capitalise on it — at that stage, on a spurious supposition that you could actually get a title for it.'

It was 1987 and Bruce had advertised it nationally, hoping 'yuppies from Auckland' might come down and bid in the $200,000 range for it. In the meantime, Lynne and Peter had fallen in love with it.

'I came over for the auction with Lynne,' Peter tells me. 'I was not very experienced at auctions and so it got passed in. Then Lynne gave me a jab in the ribs and I put my finger up. We bought it for $31,000. Back then, a pretty flash house in Greymouth was $25,000. So it did seem to be a little bit expensive, but in comparison to a shitty little apartment in North Riccarton, where my parents lived, which fetched $70,000, it seemed like a steal.'

Lynne points out, with a smile, that at that stage the bach didn't even have a title.

'Yes, it had no title, but that never worried me,' Peter says.

PREVIOUS SPREAD
Sinclair's Bach juts out into the Tasman Sea like a ship that's run aground on the rocks.

ABOVE
Lynne and Peter.

OPPOSITE
Dinner time in the conservatory.

The windows may not all be straight.

Multiple renovations have transformed the bach into a comfortable beach dwelling.

A local MP put through a private members' bill, which allowed for the establishment of title for the 36 properties on the seaward side of the road between Greymouth and the Buller Line.

'Buller, of course, didn't bother about all these hippies living in places,' Peter says. 'They just sent the bulldozers in and took them down. But nobody ever did that in Greymouth. And while we were away in France, some of the locals got together and said, "Hey, let's do it." And they did — they made it possible to establish title, and we did that when we came back.'

Peter's father, George, was the leader of the band George Crowe and The Blue Mariners. Peter changed his last name to Laurence in the 1980s.

Peter, 69, first visited the coast with his parents when they arrived in New Zealand around 1961. They travelled all the way from Greymouth to Westport. He remembers there were 200 metres of tar-seal up at Punakaiki, in front of the shop, and the rest of it was shingle.

'We think the first dwelling was built on the site in 1896,' he says. 'We had a centenary party in 1996. There's been some kind of property on this site ever since.'

Bruce Sinclair owned it for 15 years before Peter and Lynne. He was an art teacher at Greymouth High School. It is said that he did a lot of the extensions by painting the timber black so nobody could see any work was being done on the dwelling.

'He's the one who put the windows in and you'll notice the long one above the kitchen is not straight because he put the windows in before he repiled it,' Lynne laughs. 'There's a slight slope on the ceiling and an angle on the window and the straight shelf below it. It's quite subtle, but it's enough to make you think that you probably don't need another drink.'

Up until Covid, Peter and Lynne would split their time between France, New Zealand and Italy. Before Peter met Lynne, he worked in the oil industry and had 'so much money that it was coming out of my ears'. By the time he met Lynne, he'd quit and was working as a stonemason.

Lynne rolls her eyes in jest, and tells me she always had terrible timing. She would visit France regularly with Peter, who had an EU passport. They restored a fourteenth-century village house in France and one in Italy.

With their travel and passion for Europe, they decided to share their bach at 14 Mile.

'Every man and his dog has had some time in this place,' Peter laughs. 'We actually like sharing it, because it is special, isn't it? It doesn't take anything away from it to let other people enjoy it.'

Lynne tells me that Bruce always thought the bach sat on a significant ley line. One night sticks in her mind more than any other.

'I was lying in bed there and I never pull the curtains — you don't need to here,' she says. 'All of a sudden, there's a storm going on, and I swear a bolt of lightning came through the window above my bed and out the other one. I pulled my head under the blankets and went back to sleep again. I might have been dreaming but I don't think so. I am absolutely convinced that happened.

'If you get a really hefty storm, these windows actually bow in and out,' she tells me, pointing to the front windows. 'So you pull the blinds down so you can't see that. And you go in the bottom bunk in the bunk room — it's got a big rock on the side of the house there. You feel as safe as houses. You might not be, but it doesn't matter; you feel as if you

are. The roar of that ocean can be deafening —
you can hear those huge rocks rolling around
when it really gets going.'

Along with a plentiful supply of seafood,
the beach also has a surf break 200 metres
north of the bach. It's not one of the best
breaks along the coast, but always has a few
surfers when conditions are good.

The beach first gained notoriety as a beach
claim for gold — the claim came with the bach.

'I think there was an old riffle box
somewhere, but that's long gone,' Peter says.
'The trouble with beach gold is that it's so
fine you really need mercury to recover it.
You need felt in the tray and then you wash
that out and you put that through mercury to
recover the gold. That was the original reason

for having a place on the rocks — for the gold.'

Every year, a university's geology
department does a field trip to the beach. The
rock is the most solid rock on the whole coast.

'Those fingers out there, that's volcanic
basalt,' Peter explains. 'It's come out of a
fissure in a volcano. The bit that matches
that is now in Northwest Nelson Forest Park
[Kahurangi National Park as of 1996]. This is
the very hardest rock anywhere on the coast.'

'I thought I'd died and gone to heaven,'
Lynne smiles. 'I woke up and the whole beach
was full of young men. There I was in my
pyjamas, with my cup of coffee. They were
everywhere and I had no idea what was going
on, so I had to quickly come in and make
myself look a wee bit more respectable. I went

down there and asked them, "What are you doing?"'

Peter admitted he would have been happy to retire here, but Lynne wasn't so keen. They came to the conclusion that it wouldn't be a 'suitable place for us to come and make old bones'. The maintenance is constant and similar to what you might expect on a ship.

'I thought, *Well, an army only marches at the speed of its slowest soldier and if she's not happy, we're not going to be happy here*,' Peter says.

'I am not going back to last-hand cars,' Lynne smiles. 'When we lived here, we had to have last-hand cars. They'd sit out there for a while and they'd be rusting. You could see them rusting before your eyes.'

'You know second-hand cars?' Peter asks.

'Well, we had last-hand cars — after us it was the tip.'

—

Lynne was born in Kumara, south of Greymouth. She is a fourth-generation coaster. When she turned eight, her family left Kumara and went to Christchurch. Lynne went from a two-room school in Kumara to Fendalton Primary School. She hated the move.

After leaving school, Lynne worked as a legal executive in Christchurch with one of the big law firms.

'I was the death department. I did the estates, wills and trusts — things like that. It was interesting. I really liked it, but it was demanding. Every six minutes on your time sheet, every day. They knew when you sneezed, and you had fee targets to meet all the time.'

Lynne had a son who grew up in Christchurch. She also met Peter there — they married in 1990. Once Lynne's son had left home, Peter suggested she quit her job and move to France.

'That was a bit of a culture shock,' she recalls. 'I'd done a bit of French in school, but I couldn't speak it. So I was over there being treated a bit like I was ten years old by a lot of people. I remember a ten-year-old asking Peter, "What's wrong with Lynne? She doesn't talk properly." That was a whole different thing; going from being invited to cocktail parties and posh places all over the place, being treated as somebody who was reasonably intelligent, and then all of a sudden you're dumb. Some days, I just didn't want to go out. But then I started laughing at their jokes and they thought, *She does understand after all*. It comes.'

Peter was fluent — he'd had five years studying French at school, a couple at university and he'd worked there for 10 years.

'I speak quite a few languages,' he explains. 'Not all of them very well, but enough to get by. I can speak Indonesian and I'm fluent in French, Italian and English. I used to speak really good Russian, but I haven't spoken that for some time. I can speak Thai, Malay, Japanese, a bit of Batak, Arab and a bit of Ukrainian, but not much.'

'That's about it,' Lynne says, ending his run with a grin.

'Spanish? No, not really. I can get by,' he adds.

'No, don't try and stretch it,' Lynne laughs.

Peter says he learnt these languages through 40 years of working with people who didn't speak English.

'What are you going to do?' he asks. 'You can try speaking slowly and loudly in English and it's not going to work. It never worked for me, so I just figured that I had to learn the language. I've always had a real interest in it because travelling for us is an end in itself. It's not a holiday; it's something else. And if you're going to travel like that, if you can talk to people, it's a much more meaningful experience.'

—

Once they had bought Sinclair's Bach, they had to decide what to do with it. The structure's footprint was complete and the aluminium windows were in place.

'It was logs and planks and building paper,' Peter says. 'There was a parachute in front of the fireplace lining the ceiling. And in one corner, there was a dentist's chair. And there was a Chinaman potbelly in another. And out the back there was this big, round bath. The

OPPOSITE
Peter and Lynne enjoy a wine at their bach.

Lorenzo unwinds near the fire.

NEXT SPREAD
The bach's volcanic foundations run out into the Tasman Sea.

toilet was there, but there was no shower. The
kitchen had one cold tap and a bench. And
that was about it.'

Lynne describes it as 'primitive', with
no floor in the bunkroom, just some planks
across.

'It was a work in progress, and I thought,
Well, it's just great the way it is,' Peter laughs.
'And Lynne said, "No, we've really got to
finish it." So we gibbed, we insulated, we
wired, we plumbed, we painted and we
furnished . . . and here it is.'

'Then we got on a plane and went to
France,' Lynne laughs. 'We knew the bach
would always be there for us.'

Lynne and Peter would retreat to France
for New Zealand's winter and return in
summer, apart from one three-year stint they
did in France. They made the decision to rent
the bach out.

'There has always been somebody living in
it,' Peter says. 'One time, we let it to somebody
and when we came back there was somebody
else who we hadn't met living in here.'

Over the years, the West Coast has grown
more popular. When they first moved in, if
there was a car coming along the road, they'd
run out to see who it was. These days State
Highway 6 is very busy.

'It's kind of New Zealand's Route 66,
because it starts at Bluff and it goes all the
way through to a nondescript intersection
in Blenheim,' Peter tells me. 'It's the second-
longest national highway in the country. I've
always loved the road itself. I've got a love
affair with the road — I always have had.'

Peter loves his cars and races classic and
vintage bikes. In Greymouth, he has a shed
full of them in various states of assembly.

'The drive from Greymouth to Westport
is considered one of the classic drives to do,'
Peter says. 'It's not all brilliant. Some of it's a

bit ho-hum, but it's still pretty nice.'

Lynne tells me that travelling slowly through an area is the best way to travel, and she should know; she once walked every track accessible from the West Coast for a job.

'It was the job to die for,' she says. 'I was working at the visitor centre in Punakaiki, and in the winter the people who were on short contracts were sometimes let go. And I thought, *Oh well, there's me gone for the winter*. But they needed people to walk all the tracks and measure the bridges and walkways.

'I went with eleven blokes, lucky me, to walk all the tracks from Karamea to Haast.

'It was bloody cold some of the time, but it was magic. I came back as fit as I've ever been, and went to all these lovely places that I'd not

been before. You're wet and cold and getting paid for it. That's the best job I've ever had.'

After his time working in the oil industry and then as a stonemason, Peter now uses his linguistic skills at sea, working with a Korean company. He monitors their fishing boats and does Maritime New Zealand training for them. He's just got back from a 46-day stint at sea with just one week's break in between.

'They always have issues on the boats,' Peter says. 'I'm not an observer for government. I'm there to do the company business — whatever issues the company has, training and reporting. Last time, I had to rewrite their emergency procedure manuals for them, which had to be done in Indonesian, Korean and English. I could have a job for life,

Peter and Lynne's bach is an icon of the West Coast.

because there's nobody else in the country who can do it.'

—

Peter and Lynne tell me that they recently made the decision to pass Sinclair's Bach on to its next owners.

'There's a big magnet in this place for us,' Lynne says. 'It's very hard to let go. But we've sold it to some people who said we could come back and stay here whenever we like, so that sort of sealed the deal.'

Peter says the reality of owning a place like this requires people with a lot of energy and time.

'The problem for us is that it's wonderful, it's magical, it's mythical, but there's a price to pay,' he says. 'Because it's a small community, the rates are high. It's an old property and it needs maintenance.'

'It needs somebody who's young and strong enough to look after it the way it should be looked after,' Lynne adds.

Each winter, when they went to Italy, a brother and sister and their families would take over the reins. Lynne and Peter liked them and thought they would be good people to continue with the bach.

'That seemed to be the right thing to do,' Peter says. 'There's time to relinquish things, so I'm okay about that . . . with a little tear in my eye.'

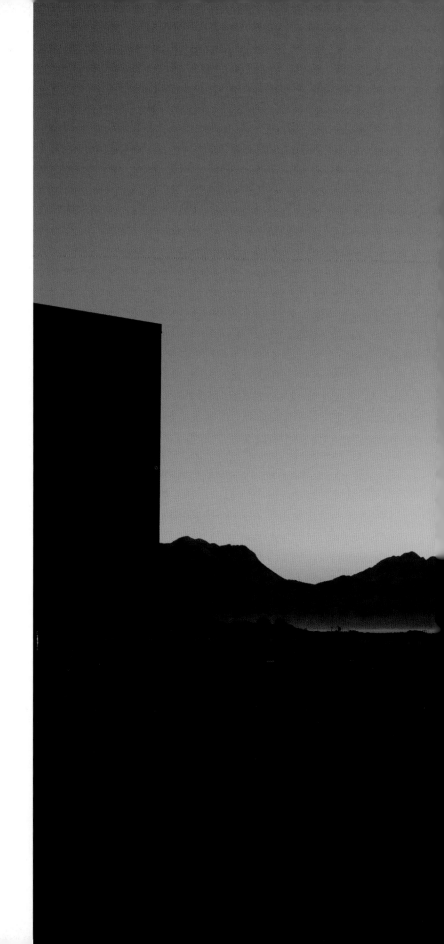

WHERE LYONS ROAM

The Lyons' family home rests on the foreshore of the Pacific Ocean, north of the mouth to the Hāpuku River, near Kaikōura. It's a timber-clad piece of art. Behind it, the Seaward Kaikōura Range pokes its ragged fingers into the sky. Snow hangs in the tops. For most people, it's something of a dream. For the surfing family that calls this home, it's a dream come true.

The first time I step foot into their open-plan living space, Dave and Cezanne are entertaining with friends from the West Coast. They welcome me in and make me feel at home. The waves that peel just over Kiwa Road from the house soon draw our admiration. The discussion turns to surf and a procession of teenagers join in for bits of the conversation here and there.

Their eldest, Reuben, is 16. He has returned from a school snowboarding trip to

Mount Lyford, which is cradled in the range behind us. He's full of energy, a great surfer and has the infectious enthusiasm of his mum and dad. His mate, Tyler Perry, is staying over, the promise of surf in the morning too strong to resist.

Their daughter, Blaise, is 14 — an equally competent surfer in her own right. She fusses around tidying the benches and putting things away, before returning to her friends.

Sonny has just turned 10 and wrestles with the dogs on the deck: Kaia, a French bulldog, and Luca, a Pomeranian—chihuahua cross who struts around like a smiling assassin. Sonny's also a top New Zealand surfer for his age, and I can see why: the backyard is some kind of surf training dojo. It has a trampoline,

a five-foot halfpipe, a slackline balance trainer and a cabana in the middle of it all that's drying wetsuits and storing boards.

Within walking distance to the house, there are four of New Zealand's most iconic surf breaks: Mangamaunu, Urupā, Meatworks and Spot X. Each of the waves is taonga to the surfers of Kaikōura — and of New Zealand.

'I dreamt of having this actual piece of land, but I didn't realise it was going to happen,' Dave tells me, as we chat over a beer in the late afternoon sunshine. 'I thought it was just a pipe dream. Then one day, Cezanne rang me up and goes, "Dave, the property at Meatworks is for sale."'

—

PREVIOUS SPREAD
The Lyons family check the surf conditions before sunrise.

ABOVE
Luca and Kaia wrestle over a bone in the afternoon light.

OPPOSITE
The timber-clad home stands perfectly between the mountains and the Pacific Ocean.

Dave was born in Auckland and went to Arahoe Primary School, near Titirangi, until he was about eight years old. Then his dad took a job as a travelling salesman for the clothing company DIC. The family bounced from Auckland to Christchurch, Christchurch to Invercargill, and Invercargill to Hamilton, until Dave was 14. Then they headed to Australia, to Brunswick Heads on the Gold Coast, for about five months, before returning to Christchurch where his father's family were all living. Dave, now 49, completed his teenage years there and that's where he first discovered Kaikōura, at 16.

'It was with a bunch of Christian surfers,' he recalls. 'They took me for a drive up here one weekend and it was six-foot at Kahutara.

I paddled out on a five-foot-nine-inch board and ended up paddling as hard as I could to the horizon. It was amazing.'

From that moment on, Dave started travelling up to Kaikōura regularly with his mates from Papanui High School.

'I fell in love with the place,' Dave grins. 'In my mind, I always called this place home, even though I wasn't living here then.'

Cezanne grew up in Kaiapoi but has had deep connections to Kaikōura her whole life.

'My grandparents built one of the first baches in South Bay,' she says. 'So we'd always holiday here from right back when my mum was a child.'

When Cezanne was 10, her dad became a crayfisherman and her family moved to

Kaikōura. She's been here ever since, and even went to Kaikōura High School — the same school her children attend now.

Cezanne remembers the day the property became available. It was 2006; Blaise was just a baby then. Initially, the owner, a farmer, had tried to sell it but couldn't find a buyer.

'They put it back to its original titles, so that made it twenty-two acres, and then all the other ones were separate,' recalls Dave. 'Cezanne pretty much said, "There's a heap of people looking at it. What do you reckon?" And I was like, "Sign it right now. We'll figure out how to buy it."'

Cezanne had seen the opportunity. They asked Matt McCory and his partner at the time, Leila, if they would go into partnership to buy the 22 acres. Together, they put in an offer.

'We were the first ones to sign up,' Dave says. 'We had to come up with a real big chunk of deposit each. Potentially, we could have lost it all. We had thirty days to come up with the rest of the money to actually buy it.

'Everyone thought it was going to fall through,' he recalls. 'We managed to secure the land. It was a miracle. It all lined up somehow.'

With the 22 acres secured, they began a long process to subdivide the property into four five-and-a-half-acre blocks, drill, sink a well and prepare their land for a building.

'It was pretty stressful,' remembers

ABOVE
The Lyons family (from left): Kaia, Reuben, Sonny, Dave, Cezanne, Luca and Blaise.

OPPOSITE
Directly out in front of the Lyons' family home is the surf break known as Meatworks.

Cezanne. 'We had a purchase and sales agreement for one block and that was the only way the bank would lend us the money to subdivide.'

They lived in the tiny little bach in South Bay as they slowly paid off the land.

'It took us ten years to be able to afford to build out here,' Cezanne says. 'It wasn't easy having a mortgage on a house and having a mortgage on the land. There were a lot of sacrifices.'

'I was working four jobs, but no one saw that,' Dave tells me. 'The first few years, I was planting trees, gib-stopping, mowing lawns and I was working as a baker — doing all four. Just trying to keep things going.'

Pressure soon reached the point that Dave considered a stint in Australia to work in the mines.

'It was just hard to make good money here in Kaikōura,' he recalls. 'I had all my tickets to operate the support trucks and I'd made a decision, which Cezanne supported. We just had my CV ready to shoot back to Western Australia when the Christchurch earthquakes happened.'

As brutal for the region as it was, it meant a flood of work for a gib-stopper and painter. Dave did three and a half years in Christchurch.

'The cool thing was that I was able to come home and spend time with the family and the kids, but punch out sixty to seventy hours each week down there,' Dave says. 'That enabled us to buy the house in South Bay, which ultimately enabled us to go freehold on the land.'

With three kids running around her feet, Cezanne was similarly pressured, but it didn't stop her business mind working overtime to solve the family's dilemma. She started a very successful gift shop called Te Aroha, which is now Jade Kiwi, in Kaikōura.

With the land freehold, they set about the house build, using the equity to get the bank across the line. But their journey was never going to be easy.

They'd just laid the pre-slab when, just after midnight on 14 November 2016, multiple faults ruptured in quick succession beneath Kaikōura. The magnitude 7.8 earthquake caused massive devastation to the region. Their house build was delayed as a result.

They were getting the build back on track in early 2017, about to pour the concrete slab, when Dave went out for a surf at Meatworks.

'It was just after the earthquake and I guess everything had lifted up,' he recalls. 'Things had slightly changed there. I was racing on a left-hander, did a re-entry and I overcooked the turn. I swung around and landed flat on a rock, breaking the L1 and L2 in my back.

'That was pretty radical,' he remembers. 'I had electric shocks up my back and was floating in with my head just above water, until I got washed into the beach.'

Luckily, it was a good break — if you can say such a thing about breaking your back. Dave would have a full recovery.

'But I had moments where I was thinking, *Oh my goodness, what have I done? This could be real serious*. But I was trying to stay mentally positive. That was a scary moment.'

Dave continued to project-manage the build on crutches, while also trying to deal with the North Canterbury Transport Infrastructure Recovery earthquake operation, which was becoming more demanding.

ABOVE
A new swell wraps into one of New Zealand's most iconic breaks: Mangamaunu.

Reuben and his friend Tyler head home for lunch after a surf at Mangamaunu.

OPPOSITE
Dave Lyons drops into a massive wave at a remote reef break during a tow session.

'We were lucky enough to be able to get the house started with builders straight away, while everything else was down,' Cezanne recalls. 'It was a little bit more difficult because we didn't have the roads for delivering all the materials. But we were lucky to carry on with our build, because a lot of people couldn't.'

In those months that followed, there were earthquake repairs and the Earthquake Commission had to come in to assess damage and repair work.

'Because we were a clean build, the builders were available right there — so we just kept going,' Dave tells me. 'That was all risky and a little bit nerve-wracking.'

The earthquake had also affected Cezanne's business and Dave was off the tools.

'It was stressful,' she says. 'We decided that we had to just carry on and do it. Because if we waited, then we wouldn't be able to get builders and tradesmen.'

They were ready to move in by October. Then the roads reopened and business started to recover. The new challenge has been operating a tourism business with Covid in the mix.

'My business is pretty much about eighty per cent tourists,' Cezanne says. 'But with Covid, it has been surprisingly better than what I thought it would be. There's been a lot of support from Kiwis in local tourism. It's been pretty good — not like it normally is with tourists, but we're still doing okay.'

'It's pretty positive, considering the doom and gloom we've been hearing,' adds Dave. 'I think we're probably way better than what we thought we'd be.'

Helping them survive has been an underlying work ethic that has brought the Lyons family to this incredible location. It lets them indulge their passion for the ocean every single day.

'We couldn't have dreamed of anything better,' says Cezanne. 'With the sea, the mountains, all the kids being able to surf. Having other kids here all the time. It's perfect for us.'

Dave says he pinches himself every day he wakes up here.

'It is like living in a dream. I love watching the sun come up, the sun setting and hearing the birds. There are not many places you can be parked up and actually see no houses around you as far as the eye can see. It has its own uniqueness. We feel super-blessed.'

The family loves that they are surrounded by the real surfing culture of Kaikōura.

'I think of it as cold-water Indonesia,' Dave says. 'Just a little bit different, with snow-capped mountains in the background.'

Reuben wanders in and tells me he loves just spending time here.

'Just being in the ocean,' he says. 'Surfing whenever I can and hanging out with all my mates. It's good fun and the boys know they can come, they can surf, stay here and hang out. We go diving on the flat days.'

OPPOSITE
The training compound
at the Lyons' home
in full flight during a
national surf contest.

ABOVE
(Clockwise from left)
Reuben warms up in the
outdoor shower after a
surf across the road.

Having a local surf
break like Mangamaunu
gives Reuben a perfect
training ground.

Sonny rides the ramp
beneath the snow-
capped Seaward
Kaikōura Range.

Surfboards are tuned
up over breakfast in the
Lyons household.

He tells me that even though he has a bunch of waves within walking distance, he prefers to drive to the spots. He has recently got his driver's licence.

His younger brother, Sonny, claims he's all about the skating and pitch-and-putt course that surrounds the property — when there's no swell out front.

'I like having the surf there and the halfpipe,' he says. 'Before, I didn't like the halfpipe; it was too scary, too big. I wanted the smaller one so I could learn tricks on it and then take it up to the big one. It doesn't hurt when you fall from the top of two-foot ones. It feels like nothing. But I fell off the top of that one and I thought I had broken my collarbone.'

Cezanne doesn't skate the ramp, but surfs when it is warm in the summer, and when it's nice and small out front. They often see whales from the house, and orca visit every season.

'In the past three years, we've had them come in right through the breakers, through the pack while we've been surfing and running the surf school,' Reuben says. 'That's been amazing — quite scary, though.'

Reuben tells me about a day recently where they had some local surf kids out on a groms' day.

'There were fifteen of these little Hector's dolphins on the inside,' Reuben remembers. 'And I just heard Mum and Dad screaming. I look out the back and there's about ten killer whales right behind us, from me to the next room away. I was like, *I know what's happening here. They're all chasing the dolphins into the beach.* I just told everyone to paddle in.'

That brought some relief to Dave and Cezanne.

'They were actually feeding,' Dave says. 'They're pretty intelligent, but they'd chased the dolphins right into where all the surf groms were. So the dolphins were literally beside them and then the killer whales were on the chase. Luckily Reuben was out there going, "No, they're feeding. Go in now." Better to be safe than sorry.'

—

Dave is like a teenager when he starts talking about surfing. He gets very excited, but he's earned the right to — he still charges on the biggest waves. Each winter, he chases the biggest swells around New Zealand and, with his tow-surfing team, explores remote reef breaks known for their slab waves.

He makes no secret of the fact that he wants to develop the acreage into a training camp for surfers — starting with his own children, who all compete at the highest level in New Zealand, and including others who are keen to develop.

'They don't realise it, but my vision is that it's all part of improving them, but it's also a fun thing to do,' Dave says. 'It's going to help their turns, head rotation, open their arms up and then transferring that out into the ocean. All board sports go hand in hand, really. They all help each other: snowboarding, wakeboarding, surfing, skating.'

—

We wake before dawn the following morning. Dave has a sniff of some special wave up the coast. The Lyons family is buzzing with sleepy teenagers, readying their boards, and a high level of excitement. Dave brews me a thick coffee.

ABOVE
The expansive rooms open out to bring the mountains and the ocean inside the living spaces.

The warm, marae-like feeling of this home means there are always visitors coming and going.

OPPOSITE
Entertaining is second nature to the Lyons family.

NEXT SPREAD
Dawn at the Lyons' place usually means a quick surf check.

He sheds some light on the wave out the front of their home that has formally been known as Graveyards. It's mainly a right-hander, described by Dave as 'a fun skatepark set-up'. The local iwi have requested it be referred to as Urupā out of respect to their tīpuna, who are buried nearby.

'It's right in front of the urupā, and it is an urupā, rather than a graveyard,' Cezanne says. 'I think it's quite important that there is a bit of a change in what people think about the area — there is more to it than just surf breaks. It's wāhi taonga and wāhi tapu, a treasured and sacred place. The area has mahinga kai — the gathering of seafood and pāua — the urupā, the marae is right there and it holds a lot of Māori history. It's a very important place, not only for surfers, but for mana whenua.

'The marae is up on the hill above Mangamaunu,' she continues. 'The iwi is Ngāti Kurī. We are surrounded by Māori land around here, and the iwi is really connected to this place. Like the section next door, right in front of Meatworks and all the terraces above where the marae is, that's all Māori land. Many of the iwi still live here. I enjoy being able to live here, to be connected to the area and to respect what goes on around here.

'Our whānau has been lucky enough to become great friends with Whaea Karen Starky, of Mangamaunu. She's an amazing lady. She might be seventy-one but she's more like a twenty-one-year-old. We really admire

her, and she has become more like whānau
over the past few years. You might see her
camping out by Meatworks now with her
mokopuna in tow, tending to cows, weaving
harakeke and practising rongoā. She's a real
go-getter and kaitiaki of Mangamaunu. She
protects and looks after the area.'

Both Dave and Cezanne have Māori
ancestry themselves. Cezanne is Ngāi
Tahu and Rangitāne. Rangitāne is from the
Blenheim—Picton area.

'My Ngāi Tahu marae is Tuahiwi, just out
of Kaiapoi,' she tells me. 'I actually do have
some whānau, or tīpuna, in the little urupā
here as well. I did know that when we moved
here, but I didn't know who. And it turned out
there are a lot of my Ngāti Kurī cousins and
relatives from both sides of my tribes.'

It makes more sense to me that their home
has the feel of a marae . . . with a skate ramp.

'It is a bit like that,' Cezanne smiles. 'People
come and go and people are welcomed.'

Dave says the dream is nearly there — but
they are still working really hard on it.

'We would like to be able to share it with
other people,' Cezanne continues. 'So that one
day people can come and stay on our land in
one form or another, especially with friends
and surfers from all around New Zealand. We
always welcome them with open arms. It's
something that we always wanted to do. Our
gates are open, camp on our land, or come and
stay. It's a great place to share.'

'But we definitely do not want a
campground,' Dave laughs.

When I ask them about their dream, they
smile.

'It's taken a few years, but we're now
feeling it. It's happening,' Dave says.

'This is the dream,' Cezanne agrees. 'I think
we're living it.'

THE BACHES OF TAYLORS MISTAKE

BOULDER BAY, TAYLORS

MISTAKE AND HOBSONS BAY,

CHRISTCHURCH

It's high tide when I first walk out onto the beach at Taylors Mistake. I'm in search of a wave that might be breaking along its northern flank, but something else catches my eye. A building of sorts sits atop a rocky outcrop. The high tide laps at its foundations, which merge into the rock itself. A path takes me beneath its second storey and gives me a chance to press my face against the window.

Bach 56 is a compact, quirky dwelling that sends my imagination into overdrive. The back wall is rock — a cave that is fused to the house like it's from a mythical world. I half expect to see a goblin staring straight back at me or scurrying up the twisting rock stairwell.

A little further around the corner in Hobsons Bay, more baches perch in precarious positions and in varying states of disrepair. Some have been bombed by rockfall from the earthquakes, others lovingly protected with fresh coats of paint.

The baches draw out a feeling deep from my childhood — making huts on the farm, exploring caves — igniting that spirit of freedom and adventure. And here they are, right before my eyes, just one ridgeline southeast of Sumner in Christchurch.

The baches of Taylors Mistake, Hobsons Bay and Boulder Bay have become icons of Canterbury. Their survival against threats both natural and civic just adds to their charm. Built in the early part of the twentieth century, they've endured wild seas, earthquakes, rockfall, vandalism and condemnation by the city on numerous occasions. More than 100 years later, they're still standing, still loved by multiple generations and wowing visitors daily.

—

I dive into my journey with the baches of Taylors Mistake with writer and researcher Janet Abbott. She was born in 1955 and her father bought Bach 2, Rosy Morn, at Boulder Bay two years later. She has researched the history of all the baches and produced a quartet of books to document and present their stories. She is deeply, fondly connected to them all.

Janet trained as a research technician and worked in the paediatric department at Christchurch Hospital. Her technician qualifications weren't recognised when she lived in London from 1981 to about 1993, so she did what every Kiwi would do — she worked for a courier company. Janet and her husband, Chris, had their children over there. When they returned, Janet retrained in art history. She taught art history from about 2000 through to 2016 and has worked at Christchurch Art Gallery ever since.

'I know quiet spaces are good for me,' Janet says. 'Chris has atrial fib, so he doesn't come down the hill or go up the hill very easily. I have a bit of quiet space over here and do a bit of writing.'

Janet's children, Victoria and James, use the bach at times, too.

She says her writing is probably her biggest gift to the bach community.

'That's important — capturing the history, making sure that it's part of the council heritage festival,' Janet says. 'The council's heritage department is engaged with the project of recording the baches, and they've helped me. We've got an ongoing debate about the age of Rosy Morn, because I reckon it's pre-World War One and the council thinks it's much later. In 1911, they put a one-pound-a-year bach fee on the baches and backdated it. So every year that your bach had stood there before 1911, you had to pay a pound for it. No one was having that. There are official letters to the council saying, "Oh, I only built it yesterday and I'm a pensioner and I fought in World War One, so I don't want to be paying any arrears." So the dates of the origins of the baches are slightly hidden under this mantle of subterfuge of avoiding the one-pound-a-year fee. You could live for a long time on a pound in those days.'

Janet's first call is to connect me with 78-year-old Max Robertson. His bach, Huckleberry's Hideaway, is straight out of an adventure novel, and it will be my shelter in Boulder Bay for the night.

'My father bought it before he was even married,' Max tells me. 'I've been going over there since I was born in 1942.'

When Max's dad, Lance, bought the bach, it was a modest single-storey wooden structure with a boat shed attached.

'In those days, there was no mains

PREVIOUS SPREAD
Janet Abbott takes a
morning paddle around
Boulder Bay.

ABOVE
(Clockwise from left)
Janet Abbott drags a
kayak from beneath
Huckleberry's Hideaway.

Max Robertson's hut,
Huckleberry's Hideaway,
sits in prime position on
the boulder bank.

The living room of Max's
1928 bach.

electricity and no mains water supplies,' Max recalls. 'We relied on candles, kerosene lamps and rainwater. It was unsophisticated, but we had a great childhood over there, fishing, sledging, playing with the other kids. I've got very warm memories of my childhood at the bay and growing up there and my teenage years — taking girlfriends over there.'

During World War Two, at the height of the Japanese invasion scare, Boulder Bay and Taylors Mistake were placed off-limits and some of the baches were commandeered by the army for use as sentry accommodation. They built three army huts at Boulder Bay as extra accommodation. One of those army huts is still in use as a sleep-out behind Max's bach.

'It's been a part of my life for a long time,'

he says. 'Both my girls and their families have had great holidays there over the years, and my two brothers and their children. It's been an integral part of our family now for four generations, and soon it will become five generations.'

In 1954, Lance decided to replace the old wooden bach, and so it was pulled down and the new two-storey structure was erected in its place. Max tells me there may have been another motivation behind it.

'I remember I was probably about ten and we were all sitting in the bach one night,' Max recalls. 'There was an absolute thunderstorm and our bach is right next to a creek, which is normally dry. My father was drinking whisky and yarning with one of the other bach

owners, Dick Bain, and as the rain grew and grew, the creek rose until it suddenly started flooding in through the side door of the bach. I think everybody was too drunk to take much notice of it. So they kept on drinking until the water level in the bach rose to the level where it quenched the open fire. At that stage, everybody decided it was time to put the candles out and go to bed.'

Max says the isolation and the lack of road access makes the nine remaining baches at Boulder Bay unique. A walking track from Taylors Mistake takes half an hour if you're a brisk walker, or 50 minutes at an easy pace.

'I don't get the boat out now,' Max tells me. 'It's too much of an effort for me to drag it up and down the beach, but I read books, do some

maintenance, talk to the other bach owners, drink beer, reminisce, tell tall tales.'

He says they have excellent fishing, but it used to be even better. Originally, the bach owners used set nets, which they would put out in the kelp to catch butterfish and moki. That was outlawed as a measure to protect the Hector's dolphin population of Banks Peninsula.

'Now the fishing is either with a rod off a boat or fishing off one of the reefs at low tide,' Max explains. 'As a kid, I remember we used to catch dozens of crayfish, which we would just boil up in a four-gallon kerosene tin, but they're pretty hard to come by now.'

According to Max, the original licences were issued in the 1930s by the old Sumner

ABOVE
Janet Abbott has researched every bach in the Taylors Mistake collection. She owns Bach 2, Rosy Morn.

OPPOSITE
Rosy Morn is a classic Boulder Bay bach, built circa 1908.

An elevated lounge in Janet's Rosy Morn bach.

Walls made of boulders are commonplace in Boulder Bay.

Borough Council, which was absorbed into the greater Christchurch City Council in 1946. For years, the Christchurch City Council renewed the annual licences for a nominal sum of about £2 a year. But that all changed in the late 1970s.

'There was a movement to remove baches on unformed legal roads of that type around New Zealand, including Rangitoto Island in Auckland', Max says. 'For years, the council made strenuous efforts to get the baches removed. But we fought a very long-standing legal battle, which cost a lot of money to retain the right to stay.'

Eventually, there was a change in public opinion, which resulted in the retention of most of the remaining baches on Rangitoto and around Taylors Mistake.

'That led to the council offering us licences to occupy for a term of thirty-five years, which was a welcome turnaround,' Max recalls.

A powerful factor in the various environment court hearings was that Lance had been issued with a building permit by the council when he embarked on the new build in 1954. The build itself was a challenge because of the access. Max's father had a big wooden dinghy with a small outboard and they used that to take some of the heavy material to the site.

'I remember we took the dinghy down to the Scarborough slipway and loaded it up with all these heavy bags of cement and other building materials,' Max recalls. 'Then Dad put my mother in the bow, and when he pushed it down the ramp it was so bloody heavy it went straight under, which my mother was not very pleased about.'

Max's dream for his heritage-listed Huckleberry's Hideaway is for it to remain in use to provide new stories for the generations to come.

—

The walk down from Godley Head, where Janet and I park the cars, to Boulder Bay is a constant reveal. Slowly, the bay comes into view through the long dry grass — first the macrocarpa, then the baches and the boulder beach.

The track narrows as it drops the last 60 metres to the baches. Janet opens Rosy Morn, flicks on the lights and her fridge. Power and a connected water supply seems incongruous with the isolation of the baches, and I jokingly accuse her of cheating.

'I don't know if you've ever lit a tilly lamp, but it is quite a performance,' Janet smiles. 'A lot of swearing goes on. They are tricky old devils. I tried to refurb ours and I've got all the washers to replace all through the system. And a new mantle and you've got to set it on fire to burn it in, but then you can't move it after you've done that because it's so fragile. So those skill sets have kind of gone by the bye.

'It was a real mission lighting the primus in the morning and having a cup of tea. I'm quite happy to turn on a switch. I'm quite happy with mains supply.'

She then tells me that it would take two minutes to reroute that spouting into a tank if she needed to, if we went into survival mode. But candles are out — way too risky. Even fires on the beach are a thing of the past.

Janet's plan for Rosy Morn is to change nothing.

'I like status quo. I want to keep it like it is — holding together with a bit of paint, a new colour every year and just enjoy it. It's part of a bach community — that's an important part of it. You can start to get the feel of the different bach communities over the years; everyone must work together to deal with

the issues that we've had, to deal with the challenges we've had. We are always rescuing people with sprained ankles or who climbed up that scree cliff and got stuck.'

On 22 February 2011, when the earthquake hit, Janet was at work at the Design and Arts College of New Zealand, which was in the old State Insurance Building behind the cathedral. She remembers all the books were falling off the shelf and she was under the table before they were evacuated out of the central city area.

'I walked back to Sumner. It was surreal. It was the last time I wore high heels to work.'

Three days later, she came over to check her bach in Boulder Bay. She remembers the rescue helicopter arriving and landing in front of Rosy Morn with the rescue dogs.

'They gave them a break from digging out the CTV building,' she tells me. 'A bit of fresh air, a bit of sea.'

Janet went to work immediately and used cement and dental equipment to fix the cracks in the structure so that the aftershocks didn't rattle it too much more.

'The key thing with a stone building like this is finding the right rocks to sit on one another. The people who built it, I don't know whether they were Scottish or not, but it is built like an old Scottish croft with the materials here. And they did a really good job of finding the right rocks to settle into one another, with that loess clay cushioning between them and just settling them into place. And it seems to be okay, but it's been moved.'

Janet's family bought the bach off Harry Reading in 1957.

'Mum described him as a filthy old man,' Janet smiles. 'He used to lay on the bunk there and shoot the rats down the other end of the bach with his .22 rifle. I think it might've been

The entry point for kayaking is in a natural harbour in the bay.

a dirt floor in those days. That corner had gaps where you could see through and the penguins had got in.'

Janet grew up in South Brighton and came over to Boulder Bay most weekends and holidays in summer, when the fishing was okay.

'Dad would be up at six o'clock in the morning: have a cup of tea, light the primus, wake everyone up, go out there and fish the morning tide, and we'd have lots of fish,' Janet tells me. 'Before electricity, we had no refrigeration, so after three days you'd have to take it all home.'

By the 1960s, there were a lot of families frequenting Boulder Bay — a generation of kids whose fathers went to World War Two.

'They just wanted peace and quiet, and there was a little bit of drinking that went on around here,' she says. 'We had loads to do because we had .22 rifles. From the age of ten, you lined up a bottle floating in the tide and you'd see if you could hit it, or we would put tins on the reef out there and you'd shoot them off. It was a very rural upbringing.'

She remembers they would use sledges to bring down bags of cement and supplies.

'We'd bring it down the gully with a rope behind it, holding it back and when it gets away on you, you just let it go. I remember my brother had all his friends over and they set up the sledge on the dry grass on the steepest bit and they decided to test it out. At the bottom, the slope comes down and then it's

cut away with a six-foot drop. It is a tank trap that was dug in World War Two to prevent the Japanese arriving and driving their tanks up the hill. So they got the sledge up, and the length of rope was just enough to stop it before the tank drop. They put me on it and sent me down the hill because I was the smallest one. And of course, at the end of the rope, the sledge stopped, but I didn't.'

Boulder Bay was home to terraced market gardens during the Depression. People would make seaweed soup by filling up wooden wheelbarrows full of kelp and water. It was a male society back then, and they would have very minimal provisions: a tin of tea, some tobacco, maybe milk powder, sugar maybe, and the odd chop or a piece of meat. They

survived on the protein they caught.

Janet's family would use water collected from the roof, enough to get them through summer. But cave baches weren't so good at collecting water off their roof because they often didn't have much of a roof.

'The men had a choice: they could either carry in water or beer,' Janet tells me. 'Can you imagine how much water the women got? Kids and veges were washed in sea water. There are other stories about people going to one of the cave baches and being offered a cup of tea; the guy went round to one gully, which had a catchment system to pond the water. He went to get the water and there were two dead hedgehogs in it, but he filled his billy up anyway, boiled it up and

ABOVE
(Clockwise from left)
Nick and Kelly Hall's bach spills directly out onto the beach at Taylors Mistake.

The cave at the back of the bach has recently been recommissioned for gatherings.

Nick and his son Munro get stuck into some maintenance.

the guy said that it was the best cup of tea they'd ever had.'

Calm, quiet and surrounded by nature, the baches of Boulder Bay exude a kind of therapeutic warmth. I'm not surprised to learn that returning soldiers who had been exposed to mustard gas during World War One were told to go and live in New Brighton and in Sumner, with a lot of them ending up at Boulder Bay.

'They came out here because they could breathe easily in the easterly,' Janet adds. 'They were all quite traumatised and had what we now call post-traumatic stress disorder. They didn't have any help with it. They brought in the beer and they drank.'

They'd walk to Sumner for their weekly groceries and return via the pub, where they'd fill up for the walk back.

'There was this story about this bloke who would stop on Taylors Mistake beach and fill his right-hand pocket up with sand,' Janet tells me. 'So when he walked around the track, if he fell over, he would fall onto the hillside, not over the cliff.'

That was the first generation at Boulder Bay and many of them stayed there during the Depression and farmed the gardens for the early crops, which they got good prices for.

The first shelters were built using dunnage off the beach — the good timber that they would throw off the boats as they left Lyttelton, before containers and before restrictions on throwing timber over the side of your ship.

'They'd arrive here and there'd be a bay full of dunnage,' Janet explains. 'None of the timber was bought — maybe the doors, maybe the windows and maybe the hardware for the doors and a few nails — but they would have spent nothing building this place. There was a culture of make do and mend. There's a very

nice quote about baches that I've stolen from someone. It goes, "A bach is something that you build yourself, on land you don't own, out of things you've pinched." It's hilarious and it's absolutely true.

'A lot of the guys in the original cave baches worked over in the port in Lyttelton. There may or may not have been a culture of acquiring necessary items from the port.'

—

In the morning, I am treated to croissants and freshly brewed coffee in the sunshine that floods into the front of Rosy Morn. I am beginning to see the appeal of electricity and modern comforts.

Our plan for the day is to walk the track over to Taylors Mistake, and I'm hoping to meet the owners of Bach 49, the McClurg bach, and Bach 56, Kia Ora Ana.

Janet is the ultimate guide. She weaves in a story of intrigue, adventure and endearing Kiwi bach culture as we scramble above and around remnants of the lost cave baches.

At Taylors Mistake, she introduces me to Nicholas Hall and his son Munro, 21, who is here to help with some maintenance, back home for a visit from university in Wellington. Nick and his wife, Kelly, also have two daughters: Ruby, 27, and Nina, 24.

Nick shows me a cave, known as Sutton's Cave, out the back, which he is part-way through restoring.

'This was the start of the bach in 1905,' he tells me proudly. 'We've got a classic photograph of three guys in three-piece suits, a woman with long clothes and sleeves with ruffled collars, and massive, long bamboo fishing poles up against the wall behind us.'

Nick says they would catch the tram from Christchurch to Sumner and then walk over the hill for their weekend fishing and hole up here for the night.

The cave hut changed hands a few times, and then George Kellar built the two-storey structure in front of the cave in the 1930s. Kelly's grandparents bought it in the 1950s. They made an addition to the lounge, which made it into one of the larger baches, and then they added a bathroom on.

'We bought it off her uncle six years ago, and we've been restoring it and loving it since then,' Nick says. 'Recommissioning this cave again is just fantastic. I love people using it again because that's how it started. It had been neglected for about seventy years or something. So to get back in here is just great, in my mind. I just love it. Everybody who comes in here gets that. Imagine the conversations over the years.'

Nick's current project is to build a fireplace in the cave.

'Every cave needs a fire,' he laughs. 'I've made the hearth and we've had a few test-run fires, but it gets a bit smoky in here, so I've got to get a flue out. The wall behind was just a bit of rubbish. So we found all bits of the baches, which are being abandoned through earthquake damage. We've got bits of those and built a wall with all those pieces we could find around the place. It's got a lot of history and it's in keeping with how all the baches were built.'

Nick is 58 and runs a business with Kelly called Box Design. They manufacture a range of letterboxes for the New Zealand and international markets. They've been running the business for the past 20 years. For the past month, Nick's been off work following an operation.

'I've been resting up,' he says. 'Between our combined families, we have five baches to maintain. We have one at Punakaiki on the West Coast, right in the middle of nowhere, and that requires a whole lot of effort to keep it up to speed. Then we've got a couple of baches at Lake Clearwater and another family bach at the other end of the bay here at Taylors Mistake. It's on the cliff above Rotten Row by itself.

'I'm bach maintenance guy. It's a part-time job. Once you do something, you move to the next one and have a go there. And then suddenly you realise that two months of your year has gone just doing that.'

Munro prepares a window frame for painting, and I can see the task ahead is considerable. Nick tells me his children appreciate what they have.

'They've been brought up with it. It's all they know,' he says. 'When you walk in here and you use it every day, you just walk into the bach and it's normal. If someone new comes along and goes, "Holy fuck, look at this place", that reminds you what it is. Munro has been in Wellington at university for the past four years, and he had his mates down for his twenty-first last year. They all came down here and thought it was epic. Little reminders like that are really good for all of us.'

The bach can sleep six people, but Nick has had some of his 'solid mates' sleep in the cave.

'It's a bit of a hard ride in the cave,' he laughs. 'When it rains a bit, we do get water through here — wintertime is not ideal. It doesn't rain much in Canterbury anyway, but if you had two or three days of rain, then little fissures in the rock above end up coming through a couple of days later. I'm trying to work out how to stop them, but I can't work it out. I've had a couple of goes.'

Nick and Munro excuse themselves to get back to work and so I leave them to it — father and son working on a family bach, doing the hard graft that each bach demands but is

ABOVE
Nick and Munro in their
beachfront bach.

The wood burner takes
centre stage in the surf
bach.

seldom the aspect that people see. Creating
memories all the same.

—

I return to Taylors Mistake in the evening for a
dusk rendezvous with Margaret Thomas, who
owns Bach 56, Kia Ora Ana. It's the bach that
really captured my imagination on my first
visit and I'm excited to hear its stories.

Margaret is 56, and her three children —
Brie, 31, George, 30, and Willie, 28 — have
been entrenched in the surf lifesaving at
Taylors Mistake their whole lives.

'Brie came here when she was five months
old,' Marg tells me. 'We lived here for five
months and then went onto a farm in Akaroa.

ABOVE
Margaret Thomas's
bach, Kia Ora Ana, sits
out over the high tide
in complete defiance of
the ocean's moods. A
public walking track runs
beneath the balcony.

OPPOSITE
(Clockwise from top)
Margaret Thomas.

The dining room and
kitchen at Marg's
beachfront bach.

The back wall of
Bach 56 is rock with
a staircase that curls
around the cliff face.

The open-plan upper
lounge, bedroom and
sunroom look straight
down the beach.

The elixir of pirates . . .
fitting, given the
location.

All our Christmas holidays, we'd pack up as soon as they finished school and we'd come here for six weeks. They were nippers in the surf club right from the beginning. And they've all competed at Canterbury level and North Island competitions.'

Marg has just become a grandma — Brie has a little eight-month-old, Koa, who will be a nipper at Taylors Mistake Surf Club as soon as he can walk no doubt.

'The whole Taylors thing really has meant that their whole life revolves around the water,' Marg says. 'If they go away anywhere else, it's always got to be by the water. It really is in their blood.'

Marg was in Shades Tavern in Christchurch, in 1980, when a chap came up

to her. He recognised her from Sumner and told her he lived at Taylors Mistake and had a bach that was for sale there.

'I said I'd buy it. I'd always wanted a place here,' she recalls. 'He said the grandson of one of the earlier owners was coming over on Sunday to buy it. So I went over and sat on the rocks. The grandson didn't turn up. They came out and said it was mine. I said I would get my cheque book and give them a deposit. And they said, "No, no. Leave it until Tuesday." And I said, "Oh no, I don't think I can do that." I thought if this chap turns up, I'm in trouble.'

Marg hadn't even stepped inside it at that point. She later learnt that the grandson had written a letter stating that he had decided

not to put his money into it. Marg has since met him and he said it was the biggest regret of his life.

'I think one day the sea will take this place,' Marg says. 'We get huge tides out here and sometimes the sea spray is right up here on the windows. And there have been times when we couldn't get out because the water was coming into the kitchen.'

Marg tells me that the windows have been replaced many times because they rust.

'We've ripped them out overnight and put new windows in. We have reroofed it several times, too.

'That is nature, really. What can you do about it? We've been fortunate enough to have had the privilege of living here for so long and

ABOVE
Andrew cools off between stints at repairing the stone chimney with cement.

Andrew Thom's bach has been in the family since the early 1960s.

it's not a place that would ever be sold — it's got to stay within the family. Whatever will be will be.'

A walking track climbs the rock to the front door and carries around past the house, but Marg says people were often too shy to come past.

'We put signs up so that people are aware that it's public access. Some people feel a bit uncomfortable about coming past. Often, I'll show people through, too, because it is a privilege for us to have this. It's not valuable monetary-wise, but it's a real privilege to be able to live in a situation like this. So if people are keen and interested then we take them through — people love it. I had a young couple last Christmas; I invited them in and the girl just burst into tears. She just couldn't believe it. She was blown away, which is how I felt when I bought it.'

Marg tells me the bach owners have fought to retain the baches, which have become an attraction to the area. The owners take their custodial role seriously.

'All the bach people are very conscious of the environment,' she says. 'I go around with a bag and pick up rubbish in the car park a couple of times a week. And when we're staying here, the beach gets groomed by us all.'

After the earthquake, Marg feared the worst and promptly visited the bach.

'There was nothing. Nothing had fallen down or anything. Up the hill, my house was really badly damaged, and it was a brand-new pole house. The construction was great, but the June one just went straight through the hill and it was centred just up here. I think the cave anchored the bach. Structurally, it did well, and we didn't have any rock fall either. At the time, you could see a cloud of red dust out there. I walked outside when I was here

and that side was red dust and that side was red dust. So both ends just collapsed. When you walked outside, it was like grit in your mouth. It was unbelievable.'

She pauses for a moment as we watch surfers out the large window in the lounge.

'It is a playground for the kids,' she smiles. 'We always end up at some stage on Christmas Day here. It's probably a little bit harder now that they're older, but I think as they start to have children, they will come back. Brie, Ben and Koa have already been over a lot. They just come and go when they want to.'

I head back to Boulder Bay in the early evening darkness; the lights of Taylors Mistake illuminate the headland and beach. I will be heading out the next day and I feel a pang of sadness that my journey is coming to an end.

—

The next morning is beautiful and clear at Boulder Bay. From the balcony of Huckleberry's Hideaway, I spot another person on the beach collecting gravel in a bucket and taking it up to Thom's Bach, Bach 8.

Andrew Thom is third-generation in Boulder Bay. His grandfather, William Thom, bought the bach in the 1960s. Andrew has three kids. His eldest son, Vincent, has two children: Maya, six months, and Malia, two.

'Malia is the two-year-old little terror,' Andrew says with a grin. 'Vinny has brought them out here, so they'll be the fifth-generation. It started off with William and it's down to me at this stage. And then probably down to those younger ones shortly. Hopefully I've got a few more years left in me, though.'

Andrew has had to take some time off work as a bricklayer to help heal damage to the nerves in his left shoulder. He's using his time to carry out some maintenance and cement cracks in the chimney stack. And to relax a bit.

'I love the nature,' he tells me. 'I love everything about the place. I used to come over when my mother was pregnant with me in her tummy. Over the past thirty years, I've been coming over here regularly. I thoroughly enjoy it. It's getting back to nature, birds, fishing, swimming, peace — just a nice pace of life. It's not everyone's cup of tea, but I love it. It's a spiritual place, too, for me. I love the place and so do my boys and the family.'

Thom's Bach is one of the largest in Boulder Bay and, at 53, Andrew seems right at home perched in the doorway with a beer in one hand, watching over his kingdom.

'It's lovely, even when the sea gets big,' he says. 'It's quite a thrill when you get the big northwest swells. They crunch in and you sit here, and you see the fury of the ocean. And then the next day, the easterly or the southerly will flatten out the sea and it's just like a big pond.'

As we talk, an excited group wanders onto the foreshore at Boulder Bay — early morning adventurers who have found their way to an iconic part of the Christchurch coastline.

'It's great to see people coming over to Boulder Bay, to be honest — making the effort to get down that hill and seeing a bit of

The huts at Boulder Bay and Taylors Mistake have become icons of Christchurch.

nature, seeing the birdlife or the odd seal, just enjoying the outdoors,' Andrew says. 'Some people come up and want to know a bit of the history of Boulder Bay and they're fascinated by the baches. It's really good to be able to share that with them.'

I leave Boulder Bay via a steep track back to my car at Godley Head. I feel a strong connection to the place, grounded by the people I've met and their willingness to share the stories of their bach lifestyles with others. Collectively, the baches are equal parts a snapshot of history, a moment in time, and the promise of a truly Kiwi lifestyle for the generations to come. They're a real treasure.

FREEDOM BY DESIGN

LYNDON AND KIRSTY FAIRBAIRN

— ST CLAIR, DUNEDIN

***Our conversation is cut short**. Lyndon has been studying the tide for the past 10 years. It's about to hit a sweet spot across the sand that has built up at a surf break a mere 100 metres from the front door of his house. Some call the wave Lyndon's Left; others call it The Channel. Either way, Lyndon is its unofficial master. It's about to hit a 30-minute window when the wave will be at its very best.

Like most surfers, Lyndon Fairbairn is obsessed by the ocean. He plans his life around the ocean's tide pulses, swells and the wind that blows across its surface. Unlike most surfers, he has found a way to ensure the surf lifestyle he loves is sustainable across the arc of his life: financial freedom.

He knew early on that he would need to engineer his life to realise the future, and the freedom, he needed. Luckily, he met and married a girl with equal fervour.

Lyndon was born a few blocks away from his beachfront address in St Clair, Dunedin. He grew up in Bayview Road and started surfing when he was 11. His father and older brother had taken up surf lifesaving so the ocean was open slather. While he was at intermediate, the school went to the surf club to learn a bit about surf lifesaving.

'They had these blue boards — little blue grommet boards and we got to have a go on those,' Lyndon recalls. 'Me and my mate Tones [Tony McCombe], we just stood up straight away. And that was the start of it all.'

He said he always told his own boys, Liam, 15, and Josh, 13, about those early years learning to wrangle a surfboard.

'Tones' surfing just went through the roof,' he says. 'I was just trying to catch up to Tones. Everyone was saying, "Tony's going to be the next big thing." About two years later, I managed to get good enough to overtake him and just carried on. There's nothing quite like having a mate to chase.'

He shares that with Josh, who has a couple of mates who are streaking ahead in the surf and surf every opportunity they get.

'I tell Josh it will come, mate,' Lyndon says. 'When you're about fourteen or fifteen, that's the age bracket where you accelerate in your surfing.'

Kirsty draws from her science career and tells me that's when they get their

PREVIOUS SPREAD
The Fairbairn family home is about as close as you can get to the waves of St Clair Beach.

ABOVE
Kirsty and Lyndon hope their two boys Liam, 15, and Josh, 13, find their own paths in life.

OPPOSITE
Lyndon cooks up some eye fillet on the balcony.

The family enjoys entertaining in their bright, open-plan living area.

Josh practises on the skate ramp in their backyard.

proprioception, or spatial awareness; they get their strength and all of it starts to click.

Kirsty was born in Queanbeyan, outside Canberra. Her mum is an Aussie and her dad is a Kiwi with Polish heritage.

'Mum did her big OE but she probably went the wrong way,' Kirsty laughs. 'She came to New Zealand and met Dad. Then they moved to Australia, to Queanbeyan, for work. When I was about six months old, they packed up their Holden HQ station wagon with all their belongings, got on a boat and moved back home. I've been here in New Zealand since I was about nine months old.'

Kirsty spent her early years in Southland before her family moved to Dunedin in 1985. She attended Tahuna Intermediate and then Bayfield High School, where she met Lyndon in their last year of school, 30 years ago, in February 1991.

'We met at a keg party at the Tomahawk Hall,' Lyndon laughs. Lyndon went to King's High School.

'It was a Bayfield keg party, and someone let the King's boys in,' Kirsty adds.

'Then the King's boys came and got all the Bayfield girls. I don't think the Bayfield organisers were that stoked,' Lyndon says. 'You snooze, you lose.'

That following year, Kirsty started a Bachelor of Science at Otago University. They moved to Sydney in 1997, and she was writing up her Master's thesis by then.

Lyndon tells me they both finished uni at the same time; Kirsty had multiple degrees after five years and he took five years to do one degree.

'I wasn't distracted by surfing,' Kirsty laughs.

'It just so happened that with student loans, you could pull your money out and go to Bali,' Lyndon says. 'So I did that. I studied part-time for a year and did philosophy and psychology. I didn't know what I was doing. I just went to uni because everyone was going to uni, and a big thing for me was just to delay that cold, hard reality of work.'

While Lyndon didn't know what he wanted to do, Kirsty knew exactly.

'I was involved in sport at high school as a runner,' she says. 'I represented Otago a few times and Bayfield High School at national level. I'd do 800 metres, 1500 metres, three kilometres and cross-country. I was always interested in sport and I was always interested in science. But I thought I was going to do medicine; I wanted to cure cancer, but I wasn't sure if I could do six years of study. I decided to do nutrition, then did dietetics, then did a Master's and then a PhD, so I ended up studying for ten years.'

Lyndon completed a degree in commerce and operations management. He laughs and tells me that it was the easiest road to a commerce degree he could find.

'I went to uni to delay having to work, and then we got to Sydney and I started working,' he recalls. 'I was managing a Pizza Hut, and it was appealing because it wasn't quite nine-to-five, so I could surf and work.'

About a year into it, reality hit for Lyndon.

'It was like: well, this ain't going to cut it for the rest of your life and I don't want to have a job where I was only going to get three to four weeks to live my life and surf,' he shakes his head. 'That freaked me out. That's when I thought, *I really have to knuckle down and learn about money*. I got a job at the very bottom rung at an investment bank, Zurich Investment Bank, in North Sydney. I was on the phones at a call centre and I was just answering the phones about people's managed funds, their insurance. I started to learn about money.'

Soon enough, another division popped up within the bank: financial planning. The company paid for Lyndon's diploma in financial planning at Deakin University in Melbourne. That's when Lyndon started getting serious about where he was going.

'There was this daunting thing about work, which was a good motivator,' he chuckles. 'If I wanted to have that freedom to surf, then money was going to be the key vehicle to doing that. I just wanted to learn everything about it.'

Lyndon moved to another financial planning company, which established an investment property department. Helping people buy off-plan investment properties really clicked for Lyndon and planted the seed for his own company idea.

'I thought, *I want to get my own business, so I'm not doing that nine-to-five for someone else*. I would be master of my own destiny and all that.

'To actually tell my boss, I'm leaving to start up something fresh and new — to leave a job that had a six-figure salary — that was the most challenging part of the whole thing,' Lyndon says. 'I remember we had a wee futsal team, and we were playing after work and the next morning I was going in to give my resignation. I was dry retching when we played. I had a sleepless night, too.'

Lyndon reconciled his decision with the fact that at that stage it was just him and Kirsty. They didn't have kids and they didn't have a mortgage — it was the time to start something.

Lyndon paid a mate $260 to set up his website, he wrote all the content and that's how New Zealand Property Solutions started.

'I remember sitting in Darling Harbour with a business banker for a lunchtime meeting and I was talking about New Zealand property,' Lyndon continues. 'He goes, "This is great. What have you got to sell?" I had nothing. And I said, "Well, let's touch base in two weeks' time." And within two weeks, I found a developer in Auckland who was selling these off-plan apartments. I sat back down in two weeks and he bought two.'

New Zealand Property Solutions launched at the perfect time in the early 2000s. Online buying was starting to become a bit of a thing

— particularly around investment property and buying in different countries. It was new and a big growth area.

In 2005, Kirsty fell pregnant with Liam and that posed a very big question.

'We asked ourselves: "Do we want Kiwi kids or Aussie kids?" And that was a pretty straightforward decision,' Lyndon laughs.

'I could see it was going to be really hard for me to balance work and kids in Sydney,' Kirsty adds. 'It was going to be a nightmare. I was finishing my PhD. It was going to be heaps of work: driving and commuting. We moved back when I was thirty-six weeks pregnant.'

They moved back in October 2005. Liam was born in December.

In those last years in Sydney, they saved

massively and bought several properties
in Dunedin, since the Sydney market was
beyond them at that stage.

In 2008, Lyndon sold his very successful
company. He received 'a big wad of cash'
for it.

'I remember when I was a grommet, just
sitting out surfing The Channel on the little
lefts, looking back at the houses thinking, *If I
ever had some money, I'd buy this one*,' he says.
'We tried to buy it privately and thought we
were paying too much. Then the owner listed
it with an agent and we ended up paying way
more than we were going to privately.'

They bought the house in 2009; it was
tenanted at the time. Lyndon immediately sat
down with his brother-in-law, Dick Geeves,

who is a builder. They started to make plans for the dwelling. The person who built the house had the living area downstairs and a 'rabbit warren' of small rooms upstairs — where the views are — including a photographer's dark room.

'The architect suggested taking the first floor off and starting again,' Lyndon says. 'So we just built it up. We wanted the elevated views, upstairs living and downstairs bedrooms.'

They started the rebuild in January 2011 and had moved in by May. In 2018, they added an extra room for the kids and the balcony out the front.

Once the new build was complete, the home commanded a greater presence on the site and that affected its feeling of privacy.

'I feel like the worst part of adapting was when the scaffolding came down,' Kirsty says. 'Because the cover was gone and everyone could see the house.'

They have blinds along the front of the house that can be positioned anywhere from the top to bottom of the window's height. They provide the privacy they need.

'You can see the surf, but people can't see you,' Lyndon says. 'A lot of time, people ask us, "Are you ever at home? It never looks like anyone is home." And I'm like, "Well, that's exactly what I want to hear, because we're home but you can't see us." It's a corner house and it's on the beach and it's quite visible. People naturally think there's no privacy, but I think there's quite a bit.

'And I've got The Channel, which is right there,' Lyndon smiles, pointing to a wave that is peeling beautifully towards us.

—

As a competitive surfer, Lyndon worked hard. He counts his highlights as being the year he finished fifth in the Open Men's division in Taranaki, and 1989 when he made the New

Zealand Scholastics team as a 16-year-old. He would represent New Zealand at the World Surfing Championships in Bali that year.

'I didn't come from a rich family at all,' Lyndon says. 'I remember making the team and just going, *Oh, that's nice, but there's no way I'm going to Bali. That's mega-bucks.* I got home and the old man goes, "You're going to Bali." And I'm like "What the—?" I was fully stoked. That was a big eye-opener — my first trip ever overseas and it started my love affair with Bali.'

Over the years, Lyndon has won a few Otago Championships and South Island Surfing Championships in age-division groups. In 2020, he won his first National Championship when he won the Over-40s division in Dunedin.

'I've finished runner-up about four times to Ben Kennings,' Lyndon says. 'But that final was probably the toughest of the lot — I had two ex-national champs: Jason Matthews and Chris Malone, and then Alan Te Moananui. In the final, the waves came to me and it just clicked.'

Bali was always on Lyndon's radar, but when he moved to Singapore for work in 2013 it became a whole lot closer. By this point, Lyndon had set up Australian Property Solutions and was selling Australian property to Southeast Asia.

'From a business perspective, there are big opportunities in Southeast Asia,' Lyndon says. 'I was going up there every second weekend for a four- or five-day trip. Australian Property Solutions was a bigger beast — Asia really took off for buying Australian property.'

With young kids, he knew it would be worthwhile to be based up in Singapore. The world aligned when a dream job for Kirsty came up at the same time.

'I was lecturing then. I wasn't even sure if they had a uni that taught dietetics and nutrition up there,' Kirsty recalls. 'And they didn't, but they advertised for a sports

OPPOSITE
The St Clair Esplanade is a playground for the Fairbairn family.

Lyndon and Josh watch as a set rolls through The Channel at St Clair.

dietitian with Singapore Sports Council, which is now Sport Singapore. So I applied.'

That's when Kirsty met Joseph Schooling, an ambitious swimmer with Olympic dreams. Kirsty had been there for eight months working in the Singapore system, and swimming was one of the sports where she worked closely with all of their athletes.

'I was still getting my head around their carding system,' she says. 'I asked if they had a list of all their athletes, so I could see who was carded where. Right at the top of that list were three level-one carded athletes. Two of them were table tennis players and one was a swimmer. I was like, "Who's this guy? I've never met him. Where is he? What's going on?" They told me, "Oh no, he's in the States. He's fine, don't worry. He's well looked after." And I was just like, "Is he?"'

Kirsty reached out to Joseph. She met his mum, May, and his father, Colin, and said, 'There's quite a bit we're doing here with our swimming programme and I don't want your son to miss out just because he's in the States.'

At that stage, Joe was considered to be one of Singapore's best talents for the Southeast Asian Games and the Asian Games.

Kirsty and Joseph started to work together, and it proved to be a formidable combination. Because of their special bond, when Kirsty and Lyndon returned to Dunedin in 2015, Kirsty agreed to see Joseph through to the Rio Olympics. She loved the challenge.

After all their hard work, watching the Rio 2016 Olympic 100 metres butterfly final was something Kirsty describes as phenomenal — something she will never forget.

There, Joseph Schooling beat his childhood hero Michael Phelps to win gold in the 100 metres butterfly. A first for Singapore. He became a national hero.

'I was really excited at Kazan, at the World Champs the year before, in 2015, when he came third. I watched that race and he started so well, and he just ran out of gas and they caught up in the back end. And I remember the conversation with Joe after that was like, "I can help you fix that, Joe. That's what nutrition can do. I can give you more power and more endurance at the back end of a race. We've got this, we can do this."

'Then watching that Olympic butterfly final, he came out fast and was in the lead for the first fifty, which we expected. But just watching that second fifty evolve and he ended up half a body length in front of Michael Phelps and Chad le Clos, who is a legend, and László Cseh, all his main rivals. It was just like, *Oh, is he actually doing this?* It was incredible. And then those three rivals all tied for second — the whole thing's just so surreal and so bizarre, but incredible. It was just amazing.'

Throughout her career, Kirsty has worked with several top sports teams, including the Otago Highlanders and the Manly Sea Eagles, along with many Australian representative rugby league players. She has worked with various Olympic athletes who came to the private practice when she worked with the New South Wales Institute of Sport. She now works with two-time World Motocross Champion Courtney Duncan and the New Zealand Rugby Black Ferns team.

Kirsty has supported several national programmes and she currently leads the nutrition team for High Performance Sport New Zealand.

—

It's fair to say that Kirsty and Lyndon have equal drive and ambition. In May 2015, Lyndon's views on New Zealand's foreign buyer policies drew the ire of Prime Minister John Key.

'I was interviewed on National Radio by Guyon Espiner,' Lyndon says. 'It was all about overseas buyers and they were trying to discuss some new policies and whether

they would dampen interest from offshore. I just said, "Look, that wouldn't dampen it at all." Then Winston Peters picked up on it in Parliament.'

Winston Peters then asked Key if he agreed with Lyndon's comments. The Prime Minister replied, 'That is an interesting view that the gentleman might have — and I do not know who he is.' Key went on to outline the changes he'd made and concluded: 'If that is no effect, then that is a very interesting world that that gentleman lives in, but I would suggest it is one that is quite a long way away from reality.'

Lyndon laughs and tells me it is one of the proudest moments of his life.

'I said it was not going to dampen anything

and it didn't,' Lyndon laughs. 'So, John Key, what world are you living in?'

Lyndon has his own view on foreign buyers.

'I don't think it's right that foreign buyers should be able to buy a bungalow, or a bach on the beach,' he says. 'They're just taking them away from Kiwis. They're adding no value at all to our building industry or anything else. But they should be able to add to our housing supply by buying a CBD apartment, a new townhouse, as a way of getting an investment return. It would create more property for renters to live in and they'd be adding to the building industry, adding to the economy. That's my take on the whole thing.'

Having built and sold two companies,

Lyndon reached his goal of financial freedom in his early forties. He and Kirsty are now both 47.

'I have a lot of freedom now, and I've tried surfing for the past few years and just cruising. It got a bit boring,' he smiles. 'The whole surfing thing is great, but I've still got ambitions, too.'

He spends his time working on his property portfolio and developments. His boys have shown an interest in surfing: Liam's a sunny-day surfer and Josh is 'just a full grom — he loves it'.

'He's always sitting at that window, checking out the waves,' Lyndon says. 'Everything on Instagram is surf vids and things, so it's quite cool. He's just going

ABOVE
Lyndon takes flight during a trip to Uluwatu, Bali.

OPPOSITE
Dusk at the Fairbairn beach house.

An autumn squall dumps its load of rain out to sea.

through that phase that I loved, when I was going through school and surfing.'

Josh has recently started to become interested in competitive surfing, but Lyndon and Kirsty are not pushing him either way.

'Whether or not that's his thing, it'll be up to him,' Lyndon says. 'He's enjoying it, gaining confidence with the size of the waves and all those aspects of surfing. He was at Blackhead the other day and he's taking off on some solid ones with fully late drops, which six months ago he would have passed up. He was like: *I'm going.* And he's just loving it. He comes up laughing now. That was super-cool to watch. It's just good times with your kids.'

Kirsty and Lyndon agree that there is nowhere quite like Dunedin for raising a family.

'Here's number one for us,' Lyndon says. 'There's no other place.'

'They can be safely independent here,' Kirsty adds. 'You can encourage their independence knowing that they'll be safe, which is pretty cool. Josh has already told us we're not allowed to move.'

They have dreams for their boys. Mostly, they want them to find their own way in life. And hopefully it will involve travel.

'Like our Singapore experience,' Kirsty says. 'It taught us to look for commonality instead of looking for difference. And I feel like society at the moment is always so focused on looking for the differences between people. Whereas when you travel, and especially when you go to a completely different culture, you realise the commonalities; that everybody's actually really similar. You've just got slightly different norms, but you're all motivated by the same things. And that was really good for all of us.'

'The boys will get out of here and travel,' Lyndon adds. 'I hope we've helped them learn to make good decisions through their lives, give them that experience. I just hope they follow their dreams and do their thing.'

THANKS

Putting this book together has been an incredible journey that has involved a large cast of passionate people. Each has added something to the process along the way to make it possible to find the right people, places and stories.

My first port of call was my group of university friends, some of whom I have known for more than 30 years. Most of them are surfers and have spent a large proportion of their lives exploring the intricacies of our coastline. Their guidance laid down the first target group of subjects. Other individuals also contributed once they understood the concept and became eager to help find the next interview subject. Special thanks must go to Janet Abbott, herself a writer and researcher. She was incredible in opening my mind to the baches of Taylors Mistake and surrounds, stories so quintessentially Kiwi and truly belonging to a book like this.

I must also acknowledge those who feature in these chapters, for their time, enthusiasm and generosity of spirit. I dodged Covid lockdowns and weaved into family events as I travelled throughout New Zealand to document these terrific people and their lives. I'd knock on a door at the end of a long, dusty road, not completely sure what I'd be greeted with. Every time, I was welcomed into a new world. The love these people share for their place, their land and their home constantly moved me. From Robin's modest hut at the end of a Northland point to the immaculate beach house on the edge of St Clair's famous surf break, each place is a treasure of New Zealand's coast that is thoroughly inspiring.

In physically covering these stories, I must thank The North Face, who kept me dressed for every occasion in the outdoors, and Toyota, who supported my work with the use of a Highlander (yes, the dream vehicle for a surfer). I'd also like to thank Back Country Cuisine for making sure I had the best nutrition while camped out in remote locations. And thanks also to the Canon Professional Services team at Canon New Zealand for ensuring my gear was always performing at its peak.

Thank you to the team at Penguin Random House, who worked tirelessly to make this project fly — often from their home offices as another lockdown took hold. Thank you to publisher Margaret Sinclair, who helped guide this project to its deadline, editor Jeremy Sherlock for wrangling my words into something special, and to art director Cat Taylor for her beautiful design work. Thanks must also go to Lyn France, who helped me meet my deadline with her fastidious transcribing.

I'm not sure my family understands quite why I put myself through the mental and physical wringer that comes with creating a book like this, but they always support me fully in my ambition. I thank my wife, Rachael, and my children, Taya, Rewa and Keo, for their patience and unwavering support.

Thanks,

Derek

RANDOM HOUSE

UK | USA | Canada | Ireland | Australia
India | New Zealand | South Africa | China

Random House is an imprint of the Penguin Random House group of companies,
whose addresses can be found at global.penguinrandomhouse.com.

First published by Penguin Random House New Zealand, 2021

1 2 3 4 5 6 7 8 9 10

Text and photography © Derek Morrison, 2021

Design by Cat Taylor © Penguin Random House New Zealand
Front cover: Sinclair's Bach at 14 Mile, West Coast.
Back cover: Tata Bay, Abel Tasman National Park.
Frontpapers: Paddleboarding on Otago Harbour, Dunedin.
Endpapers: Dusk at Boulder Bay, Christchurch.
Pages 2–3: St Clair Point, Dunedin.
Pages 4–5: Meatworks, Kaikōura.
Prepress by Image Centre Group
Printed and bound in China by Toppan Leefung Printing Limited

A catalogue record for this book is available from the
National Library of New Zealand.

ISBN 978-0-14-377472-3

penguin.co.nz